SECRETS *of* *S*elf-
*H*ypnosis

SECRETS *of* *S*elf-*H*ypnosis

The Amazing New Technique to

- *Lose Weight*
- *Quit Smoking*
- *Improve Memory*
- *Change Bad Habits*

DR. BRUCE GOLDBERG

Sterling Publishing Co., Inc.
New York

NOTE TO THE READER

The masculine pronoun has been used as a convention. It is intended to imply both male and female genders where this is applicable.

This book does not attempt to dispense or prescribe for or treat medical or psychological problems. If you have significant difficulties in your life, it is highly recommended that you seek the appropriate health practitioner.

Library of Congress Cataloging-in-Publication Data Available

10 9 8 7 6 5 4 3 2 1

This edition published in 2005 by Sterling Publishing Co., Inc.
387 Park Avenue South, New York, N.Y. 10016
© 1997 by Bruce Goldberg
Distributed in Canada by Sterling Publishing
C/o Canadian Manda Group, 165 Dufferin Street
Toronto, Ontario, Canada M6K 3H6
Distributed in Great Britain by Chrysalis Books Group PLC
The Chrysalis Building, Bramley Road, London, W10 6SP, England
Distributed in Australia by Capricorn Link (Australia) Pty. Ltd.
P.O. Box 704, Windsor, NSW 2756, Australia

Sterling ISBN 1-4027-2184-6

Contents

Introduction

❖

THE PURPOSE OF this workbook is to remove any fears you may have about hypnosis and to teach you how to apply this natural and intriguing technique to yourself. Empowerment is always my main goal in my professional life as a hypnotherapist, and self-hypnosis will open up your world to train you to tap into the unlimited potential of your subconscious mind.

This workbook teaches you how to work with your subconscious mind to overcome habits, phobias, and other negative tendencies, which I refer to as "self-defeating sequences." Once you eliminate this tendency to sabotage your every effort to change and grow, you take that first step toward a new and more fulfilled you.

The main emphasis of this book is to train you to make your own self-hypnosis tapes to facilitate taking control of your life by properly programming your subconscious to accomplish each and every one of your goals. This training will help you put the "self" back into self-help and eliminate the many co-dependencies you are probably experiencing at this time.

You may be concerned with the time commitment required to accomplish your objectives. Twenty-five or 30 minutes of daily programming can significantly improve your life. The secret involves doing it every day. Your spare time is truly your most valuable time; it is your time for yourself. Apply it well. Set your own pace and incorporate this training into your daily life.

Self-hypnosis teaches you how you can achieve a goal, not why you can't. If you are like most people, you probably have some minor and some major projects which you would like to start working on. The first step is to think about what you want (your goal) and why you want it (your ideal). These techniques instruct you step-by-step in how to make these goals a reality.

You can learn to program the attainment of nearly anything–financial security, a home, a career, a loving relationship, or even the elimination of a habit or phobia. The more specific and realistic the goal, the easier it will be to achieve. The process of working towards this goal occurs even though your conscious mind (willpower) is not actively thinking about it.

Your defense mechanisms (rationalization, intellectualization, sublimation, displacement, etc.) function as obstacles when you try to change in any way. Whenever you say "Yes, but..." or "I'll start that diet on Monday," you are giving in to these defense mechanisms. Hypnotic suggestion acts to bypass the conscious mind's natural resistance to change and to reprogram the computer called the subconscious to permanently effect these changes.

In summary, the main purpose of this workbook is to train you to unleash the unlimited power of your subsconscious to accomplish specific goals to improve your life.

CHAPTER 1

A BRIEF HISTORY OF HYPNOSIS

❖

THE USE OF hypnosis dates back to religious leaders, witch doctors, medicine men and shamans. Soothsayers in ancient Egypt and Greece used the trance state for their various healings. The healing effect of astral bodies and magnets was propounded by Paracelsus (1493–1541). He assumed that magnets were responsible for curing disease.

Father Hehl, in 1771, applied steel plates to the naked body to elicit cures in Vienna. Mesmer elaborated on this concept and used a means of "passes" to effect his cures. He called this "animal magnetism" and the technique became the rage in Europe during the latter part of the 18th century.

Mesmer, unknowingly, established the basis for current-day group psychotherapy, psychoanalysis and spiritual (soul) healing. His later disciples were Petetin, the discoverer of catalepsy; the Marquis de Puységur, who first described artificial somnambulism; and de Barbarin, who magnetized without paraphernalia and whose followers called themselves Barbarinists. In Sweden and Germany, the latter group were called Spiritualists. Mesmerism quickly spread all around the world and lasted until about 1840, when it finally disappeared from the world of therapy.

The Scottish surgeon James Esdaile reported hundreds of painless operations between 1840 and 1850 using hypnosis while in India. In 1849, Crawford Long brought to light the fact that Mesmerism was being used in the United States for surgery. Dr. Long is best known for his work with the general anesthetic ether.

The father of modern hypnotism was James Braid from Great Britain. At first a skeptic, Braid began his scientific inquiry into the technique after witnessing a demonstration in Manchester in 1843 by La Fontaine (a Swiss Mesmerist). Braid concluded that the results obtained were not due to magnetic fluids, but that "the phenomena were due to suggestion alone, acting upon a subject whose suggestibility had been artificially increased."

Unfortunately, Braid coined the term "hypnosis" from the Greek word "hypnos," meaning sleep. When he later recognized that hypnosis was not a sleep state, he tried to rename this state as "monoideism," but the term hypnosis had taken hold on the public and the scientific community, and his efforts failed to rectify the situation. Braid's greatest contribution was his discovery that hypnosis could take place without a formal induction. This discovery was ignored for over a century.

The true founder of suggestive therapy was Liébault, whose book *Du Sommeil* was published in 1866. Liébault is known for his statement to his patients, "If you wish to be treated by drugs, you will have to pay my fee; if however, you allow me to treat you by hypnotism, I will do it free of charge!" His integrity, selflessness, devotion to the needy, and success with hypnosis attracted the attention of Hippolyte Bernheim, a renowned neurologist from Nancy, who, at first skeptical, later became an ardent proponent of hypnosis. Together they developed Braid's theories and treated over 12,000 patients.

They both viewed hypnosis as a function of normal behavior and developed the concept of suggestion. Both considered symptom removal to be harmless yet effective. Their views overturned those of Charcot, who maintained that it was a dangerous form of hysteria.

Hypnosis further evolved as a science in 1886 when Bernheim published *De la Suggestion,* in which he pointed out that suggestion was the basis of hypnosis. It was his credibility that allowed hypnosis to gain in stature.

Around 1880 however, Dr. Breuer, a Viennese general practitioner, introduced a most important innovation in hypnotic therapy that extended the application of hypnosis far beyond the mere suggesting away of symptoms. He accidentally discovered that when one of his patients was induced to speak freely under hypnosis, she displayed a profound emotional reaction followed by the disappearance of many of her symptoms. When Freud's attention was drawn to this case, he joined Breuer in investigating it more fully and succeeded in confirming his results. The importance of this discovery lies in the subsequent change in emphasis in hypnotic therapy from the direct removal of symptoms to the elimination of their apparent causes.

Later, Freud gave up on hypnosis and developed free-association and psychoanalysis. This was primarily because he was not able to induce deep trances in many of his patients. His own ego worked against the field of hypnosis in that he disparaged the entire discipline of hypnotic suggestion.

The need for rapid treatment of war neuroses during World Wars One and Two and the Korean conflict led to a tremendous interest in hypnotherapy. The merger of hypnotic techniques with psychiatry was one of the important advances to come out of these conflicts.

On September 13, 1958, the Council on Mental Health of the American Medical Association formally accepted hypnosis and recommended its inclusion in the curriculum of medical schools and post-graduate residencies. The British Medical Association had previously recognized hypnosis for psychiatric and surgical use.

Today, thousands of dentists, physicians, psychologists, and other health professionals receive training in hypnosis. There are even proprietary schools that will train the lay public in the use of hypnosis. Hypnosis has emerged as a valuable tool in medicine and psychotherapy. Despite the many obstacles it has faced, it is fully recognized and utilized by many scientists.

CHAPTER 2

THE PHENOMENON OF HYPNOSIS

❖

TO UNDERSTAND WHAT hypnosis is, it is important first to consider the inner workings of the human mind. The mind is made up of four different levels of activity.

The first level or stage is called *beta*. This is the level of complete consciousness. We function in this level approximately 16 hours each day. The main purpose of this level is to regulate life-controlling bodily functions such as heartbeat, breathing, kidney function, digestion, etc. About 75 percent of the beta level, or conscious mind proper, is spent monitoring these vital bodily functions. Thus, only 25 percent of the conscious mind is left to deal with what we know as our conscious thoughts.

The second level is what we call *alpha*. Alpha corresponds to the subconscious mind, and this is what we deal with in hypnosis. This level is characterized by 95 to 100 percent concentration efficiency. This is far superior to the 25 percent efficiency of the conscious, or beta, level. Examples of activity on the alpha level are hypnosis, meditation, biofeedback, daydreaming, crossing over into natural sleep, and awakening. Hypnosis is a natural state of mind. It is not sleep. You are fully aware when you are hypnotized.

The next level of mental activity is called *theta*. This is the part of the unconscious mind that functions in light sleep. The term *conscious* means awake; *unconscious* means unawake and unaware.

The last level is called *delta*. This corresponds to deep sleep. At this level, the unconscious mind is obtaining the greatest amount of rest. Suggestions will not be heard at this level. This level lasts approximately thirty to forty minutes each night.

When we get up in the morning we have just gone from natural hypnosis (alpha) to full consciousness (beta). When we go to sleep at night we go from beta (full consciousness) to alpha (natural hypnosis) to theta (light sleep) to delta (deep sleep) to theta (light sleep) to alpha, and the cycle repeats itself.

THE EXPERIENCE OF BEING HYPNOTIZED

If you are hypnotized, you will be in the alpha state. What will you experience? Exactly what is the hypnotic trance like?

Hypnosis is simply the setting aside of the conscious mind proper, and dealing with the subconscious mind directly. At no time will you be asleep.

When we are functioning at full consciousness (beta), both the subconscious and the conscious mind proper are functioning. The physical experience in hypnosis will be identical to that of full consciousness, with three exceptions.

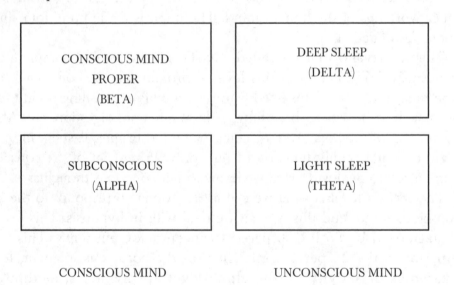

CONSCIOUS MIND PROPER (BETA)	DEEP SLEEP (DELTA)
SUBCONSCIOUS (ALPHA)	LIGHT SLEEP (THETA)
CONSCIOUS MIND	UNCONSCIOUS MIND

Figure 1

First your concentration will be more focused, nearly 100 percent, compared with the 25 percent efficiency of the conscious mind proper. Second, every muscle in your body will feel relaxed. (Some people feel a floating sensation, others a warm or tingling feeling. Most people feel a heaviness, especially in the arms and legs.) Third, there is what I call "immobility." This is not technically accurate, because one is always able to move any part of the body at any time. The patient in hypnosis doesn't want to move, so he or she doesn't. Many people have compared this effect to having laughing gas (nitrous oxide) in the dentist's office. This is quite accurate because nitrous oxide will place a patient in a hypnotic trance chemically.

Thus, a hypnotized patient will experience increased concentration, complete relaxation, and lack of movement. Also, the senses are more developed in the trance state, so they will be more accurate in a hypnotic trance state. That's it. There will be no levitation, skyrockets, or any kind of sleep or zombie effect. Examples of natural, day-to-day hypnosis include daydreaming, crossing over into natural sleep at night, watching most television, watching windshield wipers on a rainy night, watching light posts or white lines on a highway at night (highway hypnosis), reading a novel and getting so involved in the plot that you lose track of time.

Think about a daydream for a moment. When you daydream you are focusing your mind on a person, place, or event that is usually pleasant. You are not concerned about the weather, what time it is, or whether your clothes are too loose or too tight. If someone were in the same room with you while you were daydreaming, he would probably have to snap his fingers and call your name to get your attention. This is the alpha state and the best example of natural hypnosis. Everyone daydreams, and most people spend between three to four hours daydreaming every day. Thus, most people spend at least three hours every day in natural hypnosis. Hypnosis is a natural and normal state of mind. There is absolutely no danger involved. In fact, without natural hypnosis, the stress in our daily lives would kill us all.

Since our senses are sharper, we are less prone to accidents or other forms of injury when we are in hypnosis. I am not aware of any instances in which hypnosis has ever resulted in either psychological or physical harm to a patient. A person who has a car accident late at night might be the victim of highway hypnosis, but only because he would normally have been asleep, but instead was behind the wheel.

THE LEVELS OF HYPNOSIS

What about the different levels or stages of hypnosis? Today scientists classify more than 50 different levels of hypnosis, but for simplicity I will divide hypnosis into three main levels.

The first is called *light trance*. In this level the patient is relaxed and probably won't feel that he or she is hypnotized. Although regressions and progressions can be accomplished at this level, the information obtained is very sketchy. In addition, when I work with phobias (fears), habits, depression, etc., this level has only limited efficiency in accepting very complex or difficult training techniques. Ninety-five percent to ninety-eight percent of the public can achieve this level.

The second level is called *medium trance*. This is the level in which I prefer to work. In this level the patient is more completely relaxed and more able to accept very difficult or complex training suggestions. At this level the patient may be aware of outside noises but they will not distract him. About 70 percent of the public can achieve this level.

The last level is called *deep* or *somnambulistic trance*. This is the level of hypnosis a stage hypnotist likes to use because one characteristic of it is "hypnoamnesia." In other words, the patient will not remember what he or she did or said in trance unless specifically told to remember upon awakening. Only about 5 percent of the public can achieve this level. This level is also characterized by positive hallucinations (seeing an object that is not really there), as well as negative hallucinations (not being able to see an object that is there).

Even in this very deep level, however, the patient cannot be told to do or say anything that is against his or her moral or ethical code. So you see, a hypnotized person is never under anyone's control but his or her own. Unless I am interested in documenting a regression or involved in other types of research, I do not prefer to work with a patient at this level. It is not dangerous, merely unnecessary.

WHO CAN BE HYPNOTIZED?

As I have already mentioned, 95 percent of the public can be placed in at least a light hypnotic trance. People often ask me to describe the kind of people who make the best hypnotic patients and those who cannot be hypnotized. The best hypnotic patients are intelligent people (contrary to the popular misconception) who have an excellent memory, can focus their concentration, visualize scenes with great detail, can express emotions easily, are not overly critical, and who can go to a lecture or movie and become so deeply involved in the plot that time passes very quickly. Children make excellent patients because of their imagination, respect for authority, and lack of resistance or skepticism. The best hypnotic patients are children between the ages of eight and sixteen. I will work with children as young as five.

Those people who usually make the worst hypnotic patients are people who have very short attention spans, tend to focus on the past and future rather than the present, are overly critical, use logic instead of emotions, have lower IQs and have great difficulty "letting themselves go." Mental retardation, senility, brain damage, inability to understand the language of the hypnotist, and overly cynical attitudes are also going to inhibit the induction of a hypnotic trance.

SELF-HYPNOSIS

When I discuss hypnosis, I refer to self-hypnosis. All hypnosis is actually self-hypnosis. It is impossible to hypnotize someone against his or her will, unless certain drugs are used, which I never recommend or use. Thus, during a hypnotic session, a patient learns how to hypnotize himself or herself, utilizing the services of a hypnotherapist. The term for this is *heterohypnosis,* meaning hypnosis by another (*hetero* means "other").

All my patients are taught self-hypnosis so that they can condition themselves for deeper trance levels and shorten the time it takes to induce the hypnotic trance. There are many ways to learn self-hypnosis, but I find the use of cassette tapes to be the most efficient. I give tapes to all my patients so that they can be exposed daily to the techniques I give them at their weekly sessions.

OUR OWN NATURAL COMPUTER

Hypnosis takes place in the alpha state, or subconscious mind, which is best described as a computer. Just as a computer is programmed or fed information, the subconscious mind is constantly undergoing a programming process. Everything that we can detect through our five senses, as well as through extrasensory perception (ESP), is permanently stored in the subconscious mind's memory bank. Since the subconscious mind, along with the conscious mind, functions for about sixteen hours each day, scientists estimate that the average human brain is exposed to, and stores, one million separate pieces of information each day.

Each piece of information is stored in what is termed a "memory trace" in the brain. If you multiply one million by 365, and then multiply this total by your age, then you have an idea of how many memory traces you are using. Scientists estimate that the average human mind contains seventy trillion memory traces. Since a trillion is a thousand billion, and a billion is a thousand million, you can see that even a 70-year-old person has used only a fraction of his memory traces.

There are many common fallacies and needless fears about hypnosis, among them:

1. The fallacy of symptom substitution. As I have mentioned, by using regression to see the true causes of a negative tendency and by using cleansing techniques to permanently eliminate the problem, symptoms are not substituted. They are permanently removed.

2. The fallacy of mind control. Absolutely nobody can be placed in a hypnotic trance against his or her will. Even a highly skilled hypnotherapist needs the cooperation of the patient in order to induce a trance. The only person capable of controlling a patient's subconscious mind is the patient. All hypnosis is self-hypnosis and is a natural phenomenon.

3. The fallacy of revealing secrets or other information in trance. Unless the patient wants to reveal it, the information in the patient's subconscious mind will remain hidden. Psychologists use the phrase "the ego cannot be detached" to describe this. For example, in an age regression if you saw yourself in an embarrassing or even humiliating scene, you would relive this scene in your mind but would not discuss it, even if you were in a very deep trance, unless you wanted to.

4. The fear of not being dehypnotized. Because hypnosis is a natural process that the mind goes through each and every day, and because we are constantly bringing ourselves into and out of trances, a patient can terminate a hypnotic trance anytime he or she wants to. Patients do not need a hypnotherapist to bring them out of a trance. I usually count from one to five to return the patient to the beta state, but this is not necessary. The patient will resume beta functioning by him or herself. However, counting forward facilitates this process.

5. The fear of not remembering suggestions afterward. Unless you are capable of achieving a deep trance, you will always remember the suggestions or scenes afterward. I always give a posthypnotic suggestion (a suggestion that is meant to work long after the trance ends) for patients to remember everything they experienced or reexperienced upon awakening. The term "awakening" is a poor one, since the patient is not asleep, but most people can relate to this description.

The only time I do not suggest a patient remember what he or she experienced in a trance is when I am working with someone who is emotionally upset and the scene is especially traumatic. If I do not feel that the patient can handle the information, then I will suggest that he or she forget it (hypnoamnesia). In any event, the patient will remember the information or scene eventually as the posthypnotic suggestion wears off (approximately four to ten days). Even patients in a deep trance will remember the scene if you give the appropriate posthypnotic suggestion.

6. The fear of regression. I know of no case where anyone has ever been harmed by the use of hypnosis in any form. I have done thousands of regressions and other hypnotic techniques since 1974, and can personally testify to the many positive benefits. In all the time that I have used hypnosis, I have never seen or even heard of a negative effect or situation experienced by a patient. In my experience, the worst that can happen is nothing, *i.e.,* no trance is induced.

Hypnosis is simply a way of relaxing and setting aside the conscious mind while at the same time activating the subconscious mind so suggestions can be made directly to the subconscious, enabling the patient to act on these suggestions with greater ease and efficiency.

Hypnosis can be described by the following formula:

$$\text{Misdirected attention} + \text{belief} + \text{expectation} = \text{hypnosis}$$

No longer are all hypnotherapists thought of as charlatans or stage entertainers. When I first began practicing hypnotherapy, patients would seek my services as a last resort, usually after traditional medicine and psychotherapy had failed. Today, I am more often approached initially, before other traditional forms of therapy are considered. Of course, I refer my patients to physicians to rule out possible physiological causes of their complaints. When the physical causes of illness are eliminated, I begin my therapy. Any therapist you consider should take this clinical approach.

I would like to end this section with a list of some of the many benefits that can be attained through hypnosis:

1   Increased relaxation and the elimination of tension

2. Increased and focused concentration

3   Improved memory ("hypermnesia")

4   Improved reflexes

5. Increased self-confidence

6. Pain control

7. Improved sex life

8. Increased organization and efficiency

9. Increased motivation

10. Improved interpersonal relationships

11. Slowing down the aging process

12. Facilitating a better career path

13. Elimination of anxiety and depression

14. Overcoming bereavement

15. Elimination of headaches, including migraine headaches

16. Elimination of allergies and skin disorders

17. Strengthening one's immune system to resist any disease

18. Elimination of habits, phobias, and other negative tendencies (self-defeating sequences)

19   Improving decisiveness

20. Improving the quality of people and circumstances in general, that you attract into your life

21   Increasing your ability to earn and hold onto money

22. Overcoming obsessive-compulsive behavior

23. Eliminating insomnia

24. Improving the overall quality of your life

25. Improved psychic awareness

26. Establishing and maintaining harmony of body, mind and spirit

CHAPTER 3

THE PRINCIPLES OF HYPNOSIS

❖

SUGGESTION CAN BE defined as the uncritical acceptance of an idea. One cannot equate suggestion with hypnosis unless it is accompanied by a diversion or "misdirection of attention." Persuasion is not suggestion and suggestion is not persuasion! Suggestions provide sensory data input or information to the higher center of the brain.

Nearly all subjects believe that their responses are produced by the hypnotist. In reality, it is the subject who involuntarily initiates the acts in response to previously experienced conditioning. Where criticalness is reduced as the result of misdirection, a suggested act is automatically carried out without the individual's intellectual or logical processes participating in the response. And when one suggestion after another is accepted, more difficult ones are accepted, particularly if the sensory spiral of belief is compounded from the outset. This is called abstract conditioning and, in part, helps to explain the role that suggestibility plays in the production of hypnotic phenomena.

Since you will be working with yourself, it is important that you understand exactly what is responsible for the production of hypnosis. Mere suggestibility per se does not account for hypnotizability, but rather increased suggestibility is a constant feature of hypnosis.

Hypnotic susceptibility depends on motivation. It is a condition of emotional readiness during which perceptual alterations can be induced.

Hypnosis is produced on the basis of misdirection of attention, belief and expectation. A suggestion is repeated over and over again; this usually leads to a conditioned reflex which, in turn, is dependent upon previously established associative bonds or processes in the brain's cortex.

The ritual of formal hypnotic induction procedure makes full use of misdirection; the key is to give yourself suggestions when your defense mechanisms are least expecting them. For instance, during induction, your attention is fixed upon your eyelids by the remark, "Your eyes are getting very, very heavy." If your eyes actually become very heavy, then you are ready to believe other suggestions that you attribute to your own "power." You may not realize that the lid heaviness actually was induced by the constant and fatiguing position of the eyes, staring upward at the ceiling. Rather, you believe that this eye fatigue resulted from your suggestions of heaviness.

Rapport

Rapport refers to the harmonious relationship between therapist and patient. Hypnosis produces a close interpersonal relationship where the "space between" is filled by the closeness of the concentration existing between therapist and patient. As a result of this special relationship, suggestions from the therapist (heterosuggestions) are more readily followed. In addition, greater attention is paid to a therapist when this rapport exists. The rapport is enhanced by the prestige of the therapist. When a subject is in good rapport with a therapist in hypnosis, he usually responds with precision to suggestions, particularly if these are in accord with his wishes and other emotional needs. When practicing self-hypnosis, you do not need to be concerned about this principle.

Catalepsy

Catalepsy is a state characterized by involuntary contractions of any part or all of the body musculature. The counterpart of catalepsy is seen in humans during fright when they became rigid as a result of an alarm reaction. Animals also go into a catalepsy-like state known as "tonic immobility" where they "freeze" in order to blend into the landscape and escape detection. This is for protective purposes. When a limb is cataleptic, it will remain in any position in which it is placed. A cataleptic limb involuntarily resists counter pressure, and this usually indicates that medium or deep hypnosis has been reached. The whole body can be made cataleptic. When the muscles are balanced against each other, certain groups become rigid without the subject's knowledge.

Ideosensory Activities

Ideosensory activity refers to the capacity of the individual to develop sensory images that may be kinesthetic, olfactory, visual, auditory, tactile, or gustatory. Any past experience using any or all of the five senses constitutes an ideosensory activity. For example, the memory of the smell of a pine tree is a positive ideosensory activity. In order for an individual to make effective use of the imagery, he or she must be involved in as many ideosensory experiences as possible. This facilitates conditioning, particularly if he utilizes his own memories, ideas, and sensations.

Ideomotor activity refers to the involuntary capacity of muscles to respond to external stimuli. This induction technique, in part, depends on the subject's being unaware that he has made such physical responses to suggestion. Little does he realize they are a function of his own thoughts in response to external stimulation. However, he thinks he is making the responses. This further heightens his belief and expectations of the success of future suggestions.

Amnesia

Amnesia may or may not occur spontaneously during hypnosis. More often it is produced through posthypnotic suggestions. When it has occurred, there is a selective loss of memory following dehypnotization. The subject is "unaware" of what has occurred during hypnotically produced amnesia; however, the recollections are only held in abeyance. Most good subjects, when rehypnotized, can remember nearly everything that happened during the hypnotic session; others gradually forget some or all of their experiences. Still others, even though deeply hypnotized, have an inordinate need to maintain control and will not develop amnesia.

Hypermnesia or Memory Recall

Hypermnesia refers to the retrieval of information or an increase in memory recall greater than that achieved at nonhypnotic levels. I have used hypermnesia for recall of pertinent information that has helped in the investigation of crimes and legal matters.

Dissociation

Though somewhat similar to amnesia, dissociation refers to the ability of the hypnotized subject to detach himself from his immediate environment. Dissociation occurs at nonhypnotic levels during reverie states, daydreaming, or when one fantasizes himself performing many activities. We use specific images to produce dissociation. This ability to "step out" of one's self has far-reaching implications for treatment of many types of problems including pain, insomnia, and sexual dysfunction.

Glove Anesthesia

The entire hand can be made insensitive to stimuli in a circumscribed area from the fingertips to the wrist. The depth of "anesthesia," achieved in good subjects is such that the area feels as numb and "wooden" as if an anesthetic agent has been injected. Glove anesthesia may be utilized for mitigating pain in self-hypnosis.

Revivification and Age Regression

Revivification refers to actual reliving of earlier events. Usually, in true revivification, all memories that occurred after experiencing the prior events are not subject to recall. In age regression or pseudo-revivification, the hypnotized person relives the past events but in the framework of present time. During revivification, there is a marked change in demeanor, and the actions are truly compatible with the age of the subject at the period he is reliving. Recall of important memories is greatly facilitated by hypnosis. Various degrees of revivification and age regression can occur simultaneously, depending on the depth of the hypnosis.

Hypnoanesthesia

Hypnoanesthesia refers to a state where the pain is there but there is no awareness of it. The degree of anesthesia is usually correlated with the depth of hypnosis and the strength of motivation. Hypnoanesthesia is not due to such relevant variables as placebo effects and desire to please the hypnotherapist.

Automatic Writing

This refers to the material produced by a good hypnotic subject able to write while he is engaged in conversation irrelevant to the material being written. The person often has no awareness at the time of what he is writing, but later under hypnosis often can make meaningful associations to the writings.

Time Distortion

Time distortion is one of the most interesting and clinically valuable phenomena of hypnosis. It refers to the remarkable capacity of the brain to "expand" or "condense" time. This dynamism is also noted during everyday experiences. For instance, time can drag on during a boring lecture during which two minutes seem like 20. Or, when one is pleasantly engaged in conversation over the phone, time passes quickly (condensation or time contraction). Briefly, one minute of brain, subjective, or experiential time can be equated with 10 minutes of world, clock, or chronologic time (time expansion). This principle is utilized in age regression and pain control techniques.

Somnambulism

This refers to one of the deepest stages of hypnosis. It is similar to the nirvana state of Yoga and the satori state of Zen and other trancelike states. This is a rare phenomenon of hypnosis. It occurs also at nonhypnotic levels in sleepwalking and sleep-talking. Often a conversation can be carried on while the person is asleep and without his knowledge. During somnambulism, the subject generally responds automatically to nearly all suggestions. Most individuals who are somnambulists exhibit spontaneously many other phenomena of hypnosis: dissociation, analgesia, anesthesia, revivification, and amnesia. A formal induction technique usually is not needed to attain somnambulism. It just occurs. Such persons constitute about five per cent of the general population. Often they are erroneously classified as having "multiple personalities." When practicing self-hypnosis, if you are a somnabule you will not remember your experiences upon returning to your normal conscious awareness. This level is perfectly safe.

Negative and Positive Hallucinations

In a negative hallucination a person does not sense a stimulus that exists, while in a positive one, the person experiences a stimulus that does not actually exist. Negative and positive hallucinations involving any of the senses can be produced in somnambulistic subjects only. These are similar to such everyday experiences and distortions of reality that occur during fantasies, reverie states. and dreams.

Posthypnotic Responses

Actions carried out after the termination of hypnosis are called posthypnotic responses. Periodic reinforcement tends to increase the effectiveness of a posthypnotic response; repeated elicitation does not weaken it. The strength of the response depends on your motivation to accept the suggestion. Therefore, posthypnotic suggestions should be in keeping with your own needs and goals. This ability to accept a posthypnotic suggestion forms the basis of the clinical uses of hypnosis.

Posthypnotic suggestions may be remembered or forgotten when the suggested act is carried out. Response to posthypnotic suggestions can be compared to the manner in which we respond to waking hypnosis (propaganda and advertising slogans); all reduce resistance and enhance suggestibility. However, ridiculous posthypnotic suggestions will not be carried out.

PRINCIPLES OF SUGGESTION AND HYPNOSIS

Law of Concentrated Attention

Whenever attention is concentrated on an idea over and over again, it tends to realize itself spontaneously. This is more effective than simple or direct persuasion, as the critical faculties of resistances to acceptance of an idea are bypassed. A typical example is the influence that advertising—a type of waking hypnosis—can have on buying patterns. The prospective buyer's decision-making is altered without his realizing that he is being influenced.

Law of Reversed Effect

The harder one tries to do something by using his will, the less chance he has of succeeding. For instance, the harder one wills himself to remember a name or to fall asleep, the less chance he has of success. Whenever the imagination and the will come into conflict the imagination invariably wins. When employing self-hypnosis, stress "imagination power" rather than "willpower." For instance, in trying to develop glove anesthesia for pain relief it is incorrect and counterproductive to suggest, "I want my hand to get numb." Rather, use a descriptive, image-oriented verbalization such as:

> "Imagine that you are putting your hand into a pitcher of very cold ice water. As soon as you can visualize this, you will feel your hand developing a numb, heavy, wooden feeling, the same as if you had been sitting on it, or the same as if you had anesthetic injected into it."

Law of Dominant Effect

This principle is based on the axiom that a strong emotion tends to replace a weaker one. Attaching a strong emotion to a suggestion helps to make the suggestion more effective. Suggestions of relaxation are increased by massage or gentle stroking. When a child slams the door on his finger and his mother remarks, "Oh, I'll just kiss it and the pain will go away," the mere touch of her lips becomes the more dominant suggestion and makes the finger feel better.

FACTORS INFLUENCING HYPNOTIC INDUCTION

Concentration

The greater a subject's ability to concentrate, the more he will relax, and the greater the probability of success of the hypnotic induction.

Prestige

A therapist who is in a "one-up" position commands respect from the subject who is in a "one-down" position. If the latter regards the therapist with awe and respect, particularly if he is an authority, the prestige increases success of the hypnotic induction. This factor plays no role in your application of self-hypnosis.

Expectation

Expectations can influence the induction procedure and relaxation response negatively or positively. Fears and strong desires relevant to being hypnotized are examples of negative and positive effects. If you have a preconceived notion of what hypnosis is like or have already experienced the procedure, the expectation influences the hypnotic induction. A thorough pre-induction understanding (see Chapter 4) will alleviate your fears.

Motivation

Lack of motivation decreases effectiveness of both the suggestions for producing hypnotic induction and the associated relaxation. The person who always wants to be in control has difficulty with self-hypnosis. This can be obviated if you are aware that you control the entire induction procedure. Too-strong motivation for hypnotization can often evoke negative responses and interfere with the induction procedure by creating performance pressure. Skepticism also interferes with the positive responses necessary for hypnotic induction. Motivation is the single most important factor in the success of hypnosis.

Imagination

The imagination plays an important role not only in hypnotic induction, but for evoking the imagery so essential for deep relaxation and facilitation of conditioning. The readier response to imagery definitely increases the susceptibility to hypnotic induction.

Age

Susceptibility varies with age. Language ability plays an important role. Since the hypnotic induction responses are evoked by words, it is understandable why children below 5 or 6 make poor subjects. The ideal age for hypnotic susceptibility is from about eight to 16, although this approach is successful at any age.

HETEROHYPNOSIS VS. SELF-HYPNOSIS

Heterohypnosis refers to the trance state which has been induced in one person, the subject, by another person, the hypnotherapist. Autohypnosis or self-hypnosis refers to the same type of mental condition, but one which has been brought about by the subject himself without the outside help of any other person.

There is no difference in the hypnotic state between that of heterohypnosis and the self-hypnosis condition. The differences that do exist are encountered in the process of induction. In reality, all hypnosis is self-hypnosis.

CLASSIFYING THE DEPTH OF HYPNOSIS

For the sake of simplicity, it is possible to divide hypnotic susceptibility into five stages. Stages three, four, and five are relevant to its clinical application:

1. Insusceptible

2. Hypnoidal—precursor to hypnotic state—no symptoms

3. Light stage

4. Medium stage

5. Deep stage

The Davis and Husband classification (see the following page) depends on a point-scoring system and is the rating scale most commonly referred to in the literature.

Posthypnotic suggestions can be effective at any depth, although the deeper the trance the more likely they are to be carried out.

If your head spontaneously rolls sideways or forward, the hypnotic depth is increasing. Shallow, diaphragmatic breathing usually is associated with lighter stages, while slow, deep, regular abdominal breathing generally is characteristic of deeper stages of hypnosis. Other signs indicative of increasing depth are the blinking and the involuntary drooping of the eyelids. The trembling of the eyelids after closure usually indicates further deepening.

THEORIES EXPLAINING HYPNOSIS

Ideomotor Activity and Inhibition Theory

Some researchers feel that the effects of suggestibility are the result of ideomotor action and inhibition; also that suggestibility is merely an

DAVIS AND HUSBAND SUSCEPTIBILITY
SCORING SYSTEM

Depth	Score	Objective Symptoms
Insusceptible	0	
Hypnoidal	2	Relaxation
	3	Fluttering of lids
	4	Closing of eyes
	5	Complete physical relaxation
Light Trance	6	Catalepsy of eyes
	7	Limb catalepsies
	10	Rigid catalepsy
	11	Anaesthesia (glove)
Medium Trance	13	Partial amnesia
	15	Post-hypnotic anaesthesia
	17	Personality changes
	18	Simple post-hypnotic suggestions
	20	Kinesthetic delusions; complete amnesia
Somnambulistic (deep) Trance	21	Ability to open eyes without affecting trance
	23	Bizarre post-hypnotic suggestions
	25	Complete somnambulism
	26	Positive visual hallucinations, posthypnotic

experience of imagining that which is actualized through ideomotor activities. This theory may account for some of the physical and psychological symptoms seen in hypnosis, but it fails to explain the complex psychological reactions elicited during hypnosis.

The Dissociation Theory

It was assumed for many years that certain areas of behavior were split off from the mainstream of awareness while the subject was in hypnosis. Thus, the individual responded only on a reflex level with autonomic behavior. If the dissociation theory were valid, then amnesia could not be removed by suggestions of the operator. Furthermore, the amnesia would always occur spontaneously.

When it was demonstrated that hypnotized subjects exhibited better awareness of all of their senses, this theory was abandoned. Although some degree of dissociation occurs in amnesia, it by no means indicates that dissociation produces hypnosis or is similar to it.

The Regression Theory

Psychoanalysts deduced that hypnosis is essentially a regression to infancy, in which the operator assumes the role of a parent. This concept implies that, if the therapist assumed the character of the favored parent, he would readily hypnotize his patient. This is not borne out by objective observations. A child who had a domineering father would be easier to work with an authoritarian approach. A permissive technique would be better suited for an adult who had kinder and more open parents, according to this theory. Not only is this not true, but for this to be an accurate hypothesis, men would be better hypnotists than women. Experimental data indicate little difference between the sexes as clinicians.

THE HYPERSUGGESTIBILITY THEORY

The fact that the attention span is narrowed to the words of the operator and, as a result, his suggestions become more effective only explains the phenomena and not how hypersuggestibility actually occurs. It does not explain the spontaneous occurrence of amnesia or other bizarre nonsuggested symptoms as hallucinations. The hypersuggestibility theory, by inference, also implies that only gullible people are suggestible. This is not the case. It has been suggested that hypnosis is due to direct or prestige suggestion involving heightened receptive states, that the effects of suggestion during such emotional states are identical with those obtained in hypnosis. As proof, the influence of demagogues on mob psychology and the persuasive effect of orators and salesmen have been compared with hypnosis. Although strong persuasion is one factor for successful salesmanship, salesmen do not produce somnambulism, actual hallucinations, or anesthesia.

Hypnosis is not a sharply delineated state, but a fluctuating process which, like any altered state of awareness, depends upon the degree of arousal or perceptivity induced by the hypnotist or oneself. The capacity to enter into hypnosis is as subjective and naturalistic a phenomenon as sleep. Hypnosis cannot be explained by any single factor, such as cortical inhibition (a slowing down of thought processes), hypersuggestibility (being too impressionable, because of prestige and status associated with the hypnotic state of the hypnotist), atavism regression (a return to a more primitive form of mental functioning), death-feint (minimal self-awareness state when an altered state-of-consciousness is experienced), dissociation (detaching yourself from the immediate environment), dependency or transference (identifying with the hypnotist as a person from your own life and trying to please him or her) because, like any behavioral process, it cross-fertilizes with many areas of human thinking.

CHAPTER 4

THE PRE-HYPNOSIS DISCUSSION

THERE ARE MOST likely several misconceptions you have about the discipline known as hypnosis. I have already discussed some common fallacies about hypnosis in Chapter 2. Before beginning any self-hypnosis, consider the theory and clinical characteristics of this experience in what I refer to as my "pre-hypnosis discussion." The following represents a summary of the major points concerning the hypnotic state.

1. *What do you expect to happen during and after the hypnotic state?* Most people's ideas about this have been derived from newspaper articles, sensationalist magazine stories, stage performances, movies, or television. They expect to be completely unconscious during the period of the trance, and to remember nothing at all of what has happened once the trance has ended.

2. *There is no real resemblance between hypnotic sleep and ordinary sleep.* Although during the induction your eyes will begin to feel more and more tired and will close just as they do when they go to sleep, yet all the while they are closed you will remain just as wide awake and alert as when they were open.

3 *You need not necessarily expect to forget what has happened during the trance once it has passed.* Since you have probably seen demonstrations of hypnotic experiments on television in which specially trained subjects

are used, you may assume that exactly the same things are going to happen to you if you allow yourself to be hypnotized. You probably expect to have a complete loss of memory for what has occurred during the trance state. Surprisingly, you will probably remember everything that has happened, but may be convinced that you never actually were hypnotized at all. Only a small percent of people are able to achieve such depth that they experience complete memory loss, and for ordinary clinical purposes it is certainly not necessary and very seldom desirable.

4. *In working with a hypnotist, many people fear losing control of their mind.* There is a widespread impression among the general public that if you allow yourself to be hypnotized, you have no choice but to obey implicitly all the hypnotist's commands. That it is his greater will-power that causes you to surrender yours completely, with the result that you are bound to carry out his orders quite automatically. This links up the next difficulty on the list—the fear of being dominated.

    If we really believed this to be true, I don't think many of us would be willing to allow ourselves to be hypnotized. I know I wouldn't. If hypnosis could only be produced through the stronger will-power of the hypnotist, it would naturally follow that the easiest people to hypnotize would be very weak-willed people. This is certainly not the case, for in actual fact the reverse happens to be true.

5. *You need have no fear whatever of being dominated by the hypnotist, and can never be compelled to do or say anything you strongly object to.* If one were to try to compel you to do or say anything deeply uncomfortable, it would arouse so much mental conflict in your mind ("I must, but I can't"), you would come out of trance by yourself immediately. No hypnotist can compel you to do anything in violation of your moral or ethical code.

6. *Anyone who can speak and read with reasonable freedom can induce hypnosis on himself.*

7. *Almost any person can respond to hypnotic suggestion to a greater or lesser degree, quickly or in a long period of training.*

8. *The "power" of hypnosis is a power of the person being hypnotized,* not *the "power" of the hypnotist.*

9. *Words have power in that they produce ideas in the minds of the listeners. The acceptance of certain ideas constitutes hypnosis.*

10. *Suggestion of the hypnotic type plays a very great part in our everyday lives.*

We are constantly exposed to it. It can be used deliberately and purposefully for our physical and emotional benefit.

11. *Do not try too hard, but be relaxed.* A vigorous effort to be hypnotized will prevent a good response as much as a strong resistance.

12. *What would happen to you if your tape broke while you were in a trance?* Don't laugh; this is a very common question. The reaction of a subject to the sudden disappearance of the hypnotist's voice (including his own voice) would vary with depth of the trance and type of condition. A subject in a light trance can awaken at will. A subject in a somnambulistic (deep) trance would either come out of the hypnosis in a short time or go into a natural sleep and be out of the trance when awakened from the sleep.

13. *Hypnotists really do not hypnotize you, and no hypnotist has ever hypnotized a single human being!* However, many individuals have entered into deep hypnosis because they really wanted to do so. Nobody *makes* you close your eyes by suggesting eye closure. You will not close your eyes unless you wish to. No other person can make you count to yourself or lift your arm if you do not wish to.

Many of these preliminary explanations can be dispensed with in the case of children who, unless excessively timid and nervous, are generally much more easily hypnotized than adults. Children are much less critical and are usually more amenable to persuasion and suggestion. You can rely almost entirely on the "prestige factor" combined with a sympathetic and understanding approach.

I generally tell young children that I would like to teach them how to go into a special kind of sleep. That although their eyes will begin to feel tired and will close exactly as they do when they go to sleep at night, it will be quite different because they will be able to hear everything that I say, and will even be able to talk to me without waking up. Provided that I have already gained the child's confidence and succeed in arousing its interest, I find that this is usually all that is required.

The time spent removing misconceptions, doubts and fears is never wasted. It will not only ensure more rapid and successful inductions, but failure will become much less frequent. The part you play in this process, however passive it may be, is critical. Without your cooperation and willingness nothing can be achieved, least of all self-hypnosis.

CHAPTER 5

THE HYPNOTIC ENVIRONMENT

❖

YOU MUST HAVE an appropriate setting to maximize the techniques and experience of self-hypnosis. The room itself should be warm (a few degrees above room temperature is ideal) and the decor should be conducive to relaxation. The walls, furniture, rugs, drapes, and floor should not present a distraction.

Odors should also be eliminated. Plants are not a problem, and if you like incense or other fragrances by all means have them available. But eliminate any irritating or pungent odors.

If you are utilizing an eye fixation induction technique, make sure the object is higher than the chair or couch that you will be using to relax. Many of my patients like to do their self-hypnosis in their bed or lying down on a couch. I recommend a recliner instead. Your subconscious mind is preprogrammed to associate lying down with sleeping, and if you are physically tired you may very well fall asleep. Recliners do not have that association and may be more comfortable for your body.

I always use music with my patients and for my own self-hypnosis. Recording your own tapes (to be discussed in detail shortly) or using professionally recorded cassette tapes is the most efficient way to induce hypnosis. Many people like to burn a white candle in their self-hypnosis room.

Naturally, the room should be as quiet as possible. Close the door and inform other people present not to disturb you for at least thirty minutes.

I highly recommend headphones when you use pre-recorded tapes. Headphones block out extraneous noise and direct the voice of the hypnotist to the subject's subconscious mind. Other recommendations for your hypnosis room are:

1. Keep a blanket by your recliner.

2. Make sure you have tissues nearby.

3. Place a portable cassette player close to your chair if you want to record your experience.

4. A metronome or a tape of metronome beats makes an excellent background for inducing hypnosis. It also helps you pace your voice.

MAKING YOUR OWN TAPES

At first it seems that the concept of making your own self-hypnosis tape requires skills and time you may not possess. It also suggests an expensive procedure that may be beyond your budget. In actuality, this is not so.

You are probably familiar with commercially pre-recorded self-hypnosis tapes. These are inexpensive and allow you to practice this technique in the comfort and privacy of your own home. Commercial tapes are fine for your initial exposure to self-hypnosis, but it is far more desirable for you to make your own tapes. You can personalize a tape for your own specific goals. It is the equivalent of purchasing a custom-designed suit as opposed to one off the rack.

On the average, it only requires an hour of your time to produce a high-quality self-hypnosis tape. You also learn more about the art and science of hypnosis by making your own tapes.

There are only three simple steps for creating your own self-hypnosis tape. The first step is the induction into hypnosis. This can be a standard one from the many examples that I present in Chapters 6 through 9. Scripts for specific goals constitute the second step, and you will find these in Chapters 11, 13, and 15. Wake-up suggestions make up the third and final step. A standardized example is given in Chapter 6.

When recording your personalized tape, speak slowly and distinctly. You may find it desirable to play soothing background music while recording your tape. The background music can be used to mask over unwanted noise—sounds of traffic or voices in another room. Sounds of ocean waves, gentle rain, or spring in the country are available on tapes and records. Other options include using a metronome or the ticking of a clock to pace your voice and facilitate the induction into hypnosis.

By playing your self-hypnosis tapes you will literally be using your subconscious mind to build your future. Self-hypnosis means that you do this building process yourself. There is no middleman because client and hypnotist are one and the same. With self-hypnosis you are always in complete control because you are the one giving the suggestions and controlling the whole process. You are utilizing more of your mind and applying it in a personal, positive way. Self-hypnosis is a learning and growing experience. It functions as your springboard for constructive change.

You affirm your purpose and goals when you give yourself positive hypnotic suggestions. Practice will soon speed up this process and allow you to become more proficient in self-hypnosis. Visualization exercises facilitate making these goals a reality. Look upon this approach as an opportunity to reprogram old obstacles into new opportunities.

The best time to practice self-hypnosis is in the early morning, immediately upon awakening. You may be a night person or you may exhibit energy peaks in the afternoon. Regardless of your biological clock, the earlier you begin your exercises, the more you obtain from them. The last thing you want to do is to give in to the natural, but dysfunctional, tendency to procrastinate. You can also use self-hypnosis at other times of the day when you want to relax and focus your energies.

When using one of my scripts or when making a customized script yourself, record these suggestions immediately after your standard induction. Depending on your pace and the cycle you choose, your completed tape will be approximately one-half hour in length. Use this tape once or twice each day for one month. Do not record a tape longer than 30 minutes.

Achievement can happen at any time. It can happen immediately or you can experience it later on. Subtle changes may usually begin in a few days and substantial changes will be experienced within a few weeks. Some people respond quickly to the message on their tape, other people slowly and carefully change and grow, step by step, day by day. Eventually you will build your confidence and write your own scripts.

Here are some additional tips for more effectively using your tapes:

1. When you are preparing to enter a hypnotic trance, do your fingers show signs of curling? Are your hands tense? Are they clenched? If so, let your fingers uncurl and relax your hands. Are your legs crossed? Uncrossing them allows for better circulation. Are there any parts of your clothing or shoes that feel tight? Loosen them for your own comfort. Allow yourself to slow down a little more.

2. If you want to take a more active part in your tape session, sit up in bed or in a chair and lie down only after the session is finished.

3. For use of your tape at bedtime, do not include a wake-up section. Simply suggest that you go right into your natural sleep cycle from the hypnotic state. In Chapter 15 I have included a script for insomnia.

4. It is quite natural for your conscious mind to wander during self-hypnosis. Do not be concerned that you might be wasting your time when this happens. You may also experience hypnoamnesia (lack of memory), and this signifies a fairly deep level of hypnosis. Your conscious mind's activities and/or state of boredom is irrelevant to your use of self-hypnosis. We only care about the subconscious.

5. I highly recommend adding music as open spaces throughout the tape. This will deepen your trance level and block out distracting environmental noises. Again, the total time, including the music, should not exceed 30 minutes.

6. After recording your script on tape, add a wake-up procedure as I have given in Chapter 6. The term wake-up is not accurate, since you are never really asleep or unconscious. I only use this term since it is so ingrained in the public's perception of hypnosis. The purpose of the wake-up section is simply to allow your mind to gradually orient itself back to the everyday conscious world.

The following script can be used to make your first tape. This is a simple exercise and includes an induction and a wake-up component:

(Ocean sounds alone for about 10 seconds, then metronome beats in the back in sync with your voice.)

"Sit back and listen to the beats of the metronome in the background. Each beat of the metronome will get you more and more deeply relaxed.

"Listen as I count backwards from 20 to 1. Each count backwards will get each and every muscle in your body so completely relaxed that when I reach the count of 1 you will be in a very deep and relaxed level of hypnosis.

"20, 19, 18, deeply, deeply relaxed.

"17, 16, 15, down, down, down.

"14, 13, 12, very, very deep.

"11, 10, 9, deeply, deeply relaxed.

"Eight, seven, six, so very sleepy. Five, four, three, deeply, deeply relaxed. Two, one, deeply, deeply asleep. 20–20–20.

"You are now in a deeply relaxed level of hypnosis. Listen as I count backwards, again this time from seven to one. As I count backwards from seven to one, you are going to hear the beats of the metronome in the background decrease in volume, decrease in volume with each count until I reach the count of one, at which time you will hear nothing but my voice. You will be in a very, very deep and relaxed level of hypnosis."

(Decrease metronome beats until the count of one, when they are gone completely.)

"Seven, deeper, deeper, deeper, down, down. down.

"Six, deeper, deeper, deeper, down, down, down.

"Five, deeper, deeper, deeper, down, down, down.

"Four, deeper, deeper, deeper, down, down, down.

"Three, deeper, deeper, deeper, down, down, down.

"Two, deeper, deeper, deeper, down, down, down.

"One, deeply, deeply relaxed, deeply, deeply asleep. 20–20–20.

"You are now in a deeply relaxed level of hypnosis. The repetition of the number 20 three times in succession by my voice or your voice will put you into this nice deep level of hypnosis quickly and very deeply. This will get you there more quickly and more deeply each and every time you practice self-hypnosis."

(You can add whatever instructions you want to from this point on and end the trance as follows:)

"Now, in a few moments … when I count to five … you will open your eyes and be wide awake again. You will feel much better for this deep, refreshing sleep. You will feel completely relaxed … both mentally and physically … quite calm and composed … without the slightest feeling of drowsiness or tiredness.

"And next time … you will not only be able to go into this sleep much more quickly and easily … but you will be able to go much more deeply.

"One … two … three … four … five … wide awake and refreshed."

HYPNOTIC AIDS SOURCES

1. Hypnodisc—I use this in my office and highly recommend it. This is a black and green disc mounted on a stand. It spins slowly when the electronic switch turns on the Synchron 60 rpm AC motor. The rotating disc creates an optical illusion of two spirals moving in opposite directions at the same time. This also creates an illusion of moving through a tunnel and results in rapid indications. I do not know of a better eye fixation device.

2. You can buy electronic or wind-up metronomes in any store that sells musical instruments. Some electronic models have a red light at the top in addition to the audio beat .

3. Home electronic and hobby shops are highly recommended for inexpensive tie-clip and tie-pin microphones, portable cassette players, tape decks, headphones and pillow speakers (for listening to tapes while you sleep).

4. Attach a red flickering light bulb to any type of lamp.

CHAPTER 6

BASIC INDUCTION TECHNIQUES

PHRASING SUGGESTIONS

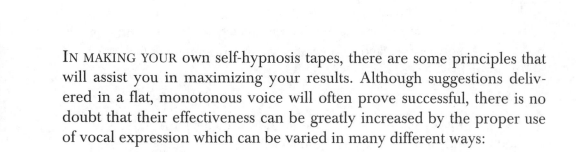

IN MAKING YOUR own self-hypnosis tapes, there are some principles that will assist you in maximizing your results. Although suggestions delivered in a flat, monotonous voice will often prove successful, there is no doubt that their effectiveness can be greatly increased by the proper use of vocal expression which can be varied in many different ways:

1. Alterations in the volume of the voice

2. Changes in the rate of delivery

3. The stressing of particular words

4. Changes in the inflection and modulation of the voice

5. The insertion of suitable pauses between successive ideas

Generally speaking, loud tones are best avoided and it is best to speak quietly and monotonously but with definite emphasis. Indeed, in most cases, a slow deliberate rhythmical delivery in an even tone of voice will often prove effective. Sometimes, however, it may be advisable to speak more quickly in order to keep your mind fully occupied. This will forestall criticism by your defense mechanisms by preventing you from concentrating too much on your own feelings. On other occasions, particularly when suggestions of heaviness, drowsiness or sleepiness are being made, it is better to speak even more slowly and deliberately than usual, prolonging the key words sufficiently to heighten the impression you are trying to convey.

In some instances, a more thorough and effective response is obtained if, in addition to quickening the delivery, increased stress is placed on critical words. But as soon as the response is obtained, the voice should once again revert to its former flat monotonous tone. This variation seems to call attention to what is happening, and exercises a powerful effect in reinforcing the idea.

THE GENERAL PRINCIPLES OF SUGGESTION

1. *Always couple an effect you want to produce with one the subject is actually experiencing at the moment.* This principle should be employed throughout all trance induction and trance deepening procedures.

   "As I stroke my arm … it is becoming stiff and straight. Just as stiff and as rigid as a steel poker. And as my arm becomes stiff and rigid … I am falling into a deeper, deeper sleep."

   And:

   "Pain is often caused and is always aggravated by tension. As you become more relaxed and less tense … you are beginning to feel more comfortable."

   And:

   "As your relaxation increases … your pain is becoming less and less … and presently it will disappear completely."

2. *It is always much easier to secure the acceptance of a positive suggestion than a purely negative one.* "I will not have a headache tomorrow" is a negative suggestion. "My head will be clear and I will feel well tomorrow" is positive.

3. *It is easier to secure the acceptance of a suggestion if it is coupled with an appropriate emotion.* We will discuss the use of visualization and imagery techniques in Chapter 12 to illustrate this principle.

4. *Suggestions should always be worded in such a way that they are both clear and unambiguous.*

5. *Overcomplication should be avoided at all costs. Simplicity is essential.* Every effort should be made to avoid confusion in your mind. The more complicated a suggestion is, the more difficult it will be for you to carry it out.

6. *The word "must" should never be used.* Avoid entirely even the slightest suspicion of domination of any kind—even by yourself.

7. *In phrasing suggestions aim for a definite rhythmical pattern, and remember, repetition is essential.* Certain words are repeated with particular stress in order to emphasize the rhythm.

   "And these same things will continue to happen to you every day ... and you will continue to experience these same feelings, every day ... just as strongly ... just as surely ... just as powerfully when you are in other places and situations ... as when you are in self-hypnosis in this room."

If you repeat these suggestions aloud, you will notice that the stressing of the word "just" serves to accentuate the rhythm, like the beat of a metronome. You will also notice that the choice of the three words—strongly, surely, powerfully is quite deliberate. The phrases not only ensure repetition, but also express the same basic idea in three different ways.

8. *No matter how deep the trance, no suggestion should ever be, given that you might find distasteful or objectionable.*

9. *In therapeutic suggestion, the most important and crucial suggestions should always be left until the end.* Start your treatment with suggestions of minor importance, followed by those of increased importance, and finish with those of greatest consequence. The last suggestions of all are likely to be most readily accepted.

10. *Suggestions should always be worded as far as possible to conform to your habits and thoughts.* If this is done, they will usually be complied with as a matter of course and will be much less prone to arouse conscious criticism.

11. *Time must be allowed for a suggestion to be accepted by the subconscious and then carried out.* It should be put in the immediate future, rather than the immediate present. To say "My headache is gone" is contrary to fact. It could not disappear instantly. "My head will begin to clear; soon the headache will dwindle away and I will feel fine" allows time for the idea to be carried out.

12. *You must have motivation to experience hypnosis.*

13. *You must also have motivation to overcome the difficulties.* It is possible to increase motivation by suggestion.

14. *If a post-hypnotic suggestion is used (most therapeutic suggestions are post-hyp-*

notic), always incorporate a cue for the termination of the suggestion if it should be ended.

15. *If the post-hypnotic suggestion should not be terminated, be very careful not to give a cue for termination inadvertently.*

16. *A permissive suggestion is more likely to be carried out than a dominating command.*

17. *Work on only one issue at a time when using autohypnosis.*

18. *All techniques utilize ideosensory and ideomotor conditioning.*

I will now present various induction techniques. Try these first and decide which you feel most comfortable in applying to yourself.

Eye-Fixation Techniques

Simply fix your eyes upon some object held above your head and slightly to the rear, about eight inches (20 cm) above your line of sight. Continue staring at it, and do not let your eyes wander from it for a single moment. This in itself will not produce hypnosis, but will enable you to fix your attention. The induction will be rendered much easier if you take care to see that your head is extended backwards.

Alternatively, you may choose a spot on the ceiling, still slightly to the rear of your head, and stare upwards and backwards at it without allowing your eyes to stray.

> "Now get as comfortable as possible. Rest your head. Rest your head on the back of the chair.

> "Fix your eyes directly above your forehead. Keep looking directly at one spot on the ceiling. Notice now that your eyes are getting very, very *heavy,* your *lids* are getting very, very, very *tired.*

> "Your lids are getting *heavier* and *heavier,* and the heavier your lids get now, the better you will relax your lids. The better you relax your eyelids, the better you will follow all subsequent suggestions.

> "Your lids are getting *heavier* and *heavier.* They are getting *very, very tired.* Your lids are getting *very, very heavy.* Your eyelids are blinking. That is a good sign that the lids are getting *heavier* and *heavier.*

> "Your lids are blinking a little more. That's right. If you really wish to go into a deeper state of relaxation, all you have to do is to let your lids close *tightly,* very tightly, at the count of three.

> "You will close your eyes not because you have to but because you really wish to become relaxed more and more deeply.

"One ... your eyelids are getting *heavier* and *heavier*.

"Two ... getting much heavier. Your lids are blinking still more.

"Three ... now, *close your eyes tightly* and let your eyeballs roll up into the back of your head.

"As your eyeballs roll up into the back of your head, notice how your lids are sticking together more and more tightly. You feel the tightness, don't you? This shows that it's really beginning to work.

"And your lids continue to stick together more and more tightly. And as your eyeballs are rolled up toward your forehead for a few moments longer, you will go deeper and deeper relaxed."

EYE-FIXATION TECHNIQUE WITH SLEEP SUGGESTIONS
This is a favorite technique of people who prefer to use the words "sleep" or "asleep."

"In gazing at that spot, you will relax quickly and deeply."

(Pause for 10 seconds.)

"Your legs will grow heavy, very heavy."

(Pause for 10 seconds.)

"Your arms will grow heavy, very heavy."

(Pause for 10 seconds.)

"Your entire body will grow heavy, very heavy."

(Pause for 10 seconds.)

"And now your legs are heavy, your arms are heavy, and your entire body is heavy. You are deeply relaxed. You are relaxing more and more all the time."

(Pause for 10 seconds.)

"You are so deeply relaxed that your eyes are now growing heavy and they are becoming tired, very tired. You will want to close your eyes. As you close your eyes, you will enjoy perfect relaxation."

(Pause for 10 seconds.)

"Deeply, deeply asleep."

(This phrase is uttered in a decisive and emphatic voice, forcefully and yet not too loud, instead of in the previous lulling and soothing tone. Repeat the phrase "Deeply, deeply asleep" every 2 or 3 seconds, 4 or 5 times. This will tend to narrow down consciousness to only one idea, namely, deeply, deeply asleep—as you will be at this point in one of the several stages of hypnosis.)

EYE-FIXATION TECHNIQUE WITHOUT SLEEP SUGGESTIONS

"I will teach you to relax. You will *relax every fiber, every muscle in your body.* When you raise your right hand, let it fall limply into your lap. Let your hand fall as though it were as *heavy as lead,* just like a wet dish towel. Your arm is completely relaxed.

"Breathe in deeply and relax your diaphragm. Again. Now relax your feet and legs the same as you did your hands. Make them *very, very heavy.* I want you to feel a very pleasant tingling, relaxed feeling in your toes. It will travel up from the soles of your feet, up your legs to your abdomen and chest."

(Pause.)

"Take another deep breath and relax still more. Again. Now relax your lower jaw … more.…Relax your cheeks. Now your eyes are very tired and heavy. They are closing, closing, closing. Close your eyes.

"Relax your forehead. Listen only to my voice. You can think of anything you wish, but you will concentrate on my voice. I want you to go into an even deeper state of relaxation.

"One, two, three,…*deeply, deeply relaxed* … every muscle from your head to your toes is completely relaxed. You will remain relaxed until I ask you to open your eyes. When you open your eyes, you will be completely relaxed and full of confidence. Each time you practice self-hypnosis, you will always relax quickly and deeply with this method. You will never forget these suggestions.

"When I count three, you will open your eyes and be completely relaxed, feeling fine. One,…two,…three, wide awake and refreshed and eyes open."

HANDCLASP TECHNIQUE

"Close your eyes. Now clasp your hands together and make them as tight as you can.

"Think to yourself, 'I would like to make my hands stick tightly together.' Keep your eyes closed until I ask you to open them.

"Imagine how nice it would be to develop self-relaxation. Now feel the pressure in your fingers as your hands tighten and *tighten* still more! Your fingertips are getting numb, very numb!

"Your hands are sticking together tightly, and you feel a pleasant sensation in your thumbs as they press down tightly on one another.

"Your hands are now so tightly stuck together that you cannot tell your left fingers from your right. Your hands feel as if they are a solid piece of wood. They are now sticking together without any effort. You have no desire to take them apart. *You don't want to take your hands apart.*"

PROGRESSIVE RELAXATION

This method depends on the induction of passivity of mind, without employing any accompanying distraction technique. It is usually preferable for you to lie on a couch, flat on your back, with your head supported by a pillow. Notice that no fixation point is specifically used. In this case, attention is directed towards a limited group of ideas.

"As you are lying on the couch, I want you to think of a pleasant, peaceful scene.

"Just picture yourself lying on the seashore … sun-bathing.

"You can feel the soft, warm sand.…You can see the blue sky,…and you can feel the warmth of the sun on your body.

"I want you to let all the muscles of your body go quite limp and slack.

"First, the muscles of your feet, and ankles.

"Let them relax … let them go … limp and slack.

"Now, the muscles of your calves.

"Let them go … limp and slack … allow them to relax.

"Now, the muscles of your thighs.

"Let them relax … let them go … limp and slack.

"And, already you can feel a feeling of heaviness in your legs.

"Your legs are beginning to feel as heavy as lead.

"Let your legs go … heavy as lead … let them relax completely.

"And as you do so … you are becoming more and more drowsy.

"You feel completely at peace … your mind is calm and contented.

"You are really enjoying this very pleasant, relaxed, drowsy feeling.

"And now, that feeling of relaxation is spreading upwards over your whole body.

"Let your stomach muscles relax....Let them go ... limp and slack.

"Now, the muscles of your chest ... your body ... and your back.

"Let them go limp and slack ... allow them to relax.

"And you can feel a feeling of heaviness in your body,...as though your body were just as heavy as lead ... as if it wanted to sink down ... deeper and deeper into the soft, warm sand.

"Just let your body go ... heavy as lead.

"Let it sink comfortably ... into the sand....And as it does so ... you are feeling more and more drowsy.

"Your eyelids are becoming heavier and heavier,...and your eyes, more and more tired.

"Presently, they will want to close.

"As soon as you feel they want to close ... just let them go ... and they will close, entirely on their own.

"Just let yourself relax ... more and more completely.

"You can feel the heat of the sun on your body.

"You are feeling warm and comfortable ... completely at peace.

"And that pleasant feeling of relaxation is now spreading into your neck ... your shoulders ... and your arms.

"Let your neck muscles relax....Let them go ... limp and slack.

"Now, the muscles of your shoulders....Let them go limp and slack....Allow them to relax.

"Now, the muscles of your arms....Let them relax....Let them go limp and slack.

"And you can feel a feeling of heaviness in your arms.

"As if your arms are becoming just as heavy as lead.

"Just let your arms go ... heavy as lead....Let them relax completely.

"And as you do so ... you are becoming more and more tired.

"So tired that your eyes want to close.

"Just let them close ... on their own.

"Closing now ... closing ... more and more tightly."

EYE FIXATION WITH PROGRESSIVE RELAXATION

"Lie back comfortably in the chair. Choose a spot on the ceiling, slightly behind you ... and look upwards and backwards at it. Keep your eyes fixed on that spot on the ceiling. Let yourself go ... limp and slack. Let all the muscles of your body relax completely. Breathe quietly ... in ... and out.

"Now I want you to concentrate on your feet and ankles. Let them relax....Let them go ... limp and slack. Begin to feel a feeling of heaviness in your feet. As though they are becoming just as heavy as lead. As if they want to sink down into the carpet.

"Keep your eyes fixed on that spot on the ceiling. And as you stare at it ... you will find that your eyelids are becoming heavier and heavier,...so that presently they will want to close. As soon as they feel they want to close ... just let them close.

"Let yourself go completely. Let the muscles of your calves and thighs go limp and relaxed. Let them relax....Let them go ... limp and slack. And as they do so ... your eyes are beginning to feel more and more tired. They are becoming a bit watery. Soon, they will feel so heavy that they will want to close.

"As soon as they feel they want to close ... just let them close ... entirely on their own. Let yourself go completely. Give yourself up completely to this very pleasant ... relaxed ... drowsy ... comfortable feeling. Let your whole body go limp and slack,...heavy as lead.

"First, the muscles of your stomach....Let them relax....Let them go ... limp and slack. Now, the muscles of your chest,...your body,...and your back. Let them go ... limp and slack....Let them relax completely. And you can feel a feeling of heaviness in your body. As though your whole body were becoming just as heavy as lead. As if it wanted to sink down ... deeper and deeper ... into the chair. Just let your body go ... heavy as lead. Let it sink back comfortably ... deeper and deeper into the chair.

"And as it does so ... your eyelids are feeling even heavier and heavier. So very, very heavy ... that they want to close. As soon as they feel they want to close ... just let them close. And now, that feeling of relaxation is spreading into the muscles of your neck,...your shoulders,...and your arms.

"Let your neck muscles relax....Let them go ... limp and slack. Now the muscles of your shoulders ... and your arms,...let them go ... limp and slack....Allow them to relax completely. And as they do so,...you will feel a feeling of heaviness in your arms. As though your arms are becoming just as heavy as lead. Let your arms go ... heavy as lead. Let them relax completely.

"And as you do so ... your eyelids are feeling so very, very heavy ... your eyes so very, very tired ... that they want to close. Want to close, now ... closing ... closing more and more tightly."

THE ARM-LEVITATION TECHNIQUE

"Would you mind placing your hands on your thighs and, if you please, just look down at your fingers, at your hands as they rest lightly on your knees? Perhaps you wouldn't mind pressing down really *hard;* if you will, just *press down hard,* just as *hard* as you *can,* as if you are pushing your knees and feet through the floor.

"Of course, this is impossible! Perhaps you can press a little harder, and still harder. And, as you press harder and harder, become aware, if you will, that you are building up a great amount of tension your fingers.

"Notice the tension building up in your fingers as you press *harder* and *harder.* Just keep pressing *harder* and *harder.* And, perhaps, you can feel an increased sensitivity in your fingertips.

"And notice, if you will, please, the texture of the cloth of your trousers. And maybe, as you keep pressing, you will notice the warmth of your body as it comes through the cloth of your trousers. And keep pressing, *harder* and *harder.*

"And, of course, you know that the opposite of the tension that you are building in your fingers is relaxation. So, any time that you might wish to relax, it is really so simple; all you have to do is just close your eyes and visualize, if you will, that one of the fingers on either the left hand or the right hand is getting lighter than all the others.

"Remember, the opposite of tension is relaxation; I am sure that you will agree to that. And if you *really* want to relax, one of the fingers on *either* the *left* hand or the *right* hand is getting lighter than all the others.

"And as it gets lighter than all the others, perhaps one of the fingers will begin to lift up in the air. And one of the fingers will begin to move on either the left hand or the right hand.

"Which finger will it be? Maybe it will be the little finger of the left hand or perhaps it will be the ring finger of the right hand. It might even be the forefinger of the left hand.

"And I notice the forefinger of the right hand is beginning to lift. And it's *lifting, lifting, lifting.* And as it gets lighter than all of the other fingers, the other fingers of that hand can begin to lift.

"And very soon, if you wish, you are going to notice the most wonderful sensation, a floating, soothing sensation. The right hand is lifting in the direction of your face. Lifting, lifting, lifting.

"And perhaps you might be willing to give yourself the suggestions that with each motion that your arm lifts upward you will become more and more deeply relaxed; your arm is lifting not because it has to, but because it wants to.

"You will soon reach a *deep* state, a *deep state of relaxation.* The right hand is now lifting, lifting, lifting, lifting, lifting! And perhaps you can visualize a balloon tied around your wrist, and now another balloon, or three or four balloons are tugging at your wrist.

"And then you can visualize still another balloon. A red balloon, a blue balloon, and your arm is now lifting, lifting, lifting, lifting.

"And as soon as it touches your face you might be willing to give yourself a suggestion that the moment any portion of your hand touches any portion of your face that will be a signal, perhaps, for you to be willing to drop into an *even deeper* state of relaxation.

"As your arm lifts, you are becoming *more and more deeply relaxed.* That's fine. You are doing just fine. You are really willing to learn, aren't you?

"Hypnosis is a learning process. And if you learn these simple, elementary A-B-C suggestions, then you can learn other suggestions that are so necessary for complete mental and physical relaxation. And as the hand draws closer and closer to the face, just think of that wonderful feeling of relaxation that is going to come over your body."

CHILD INDUCTION TECHNIQUES

When using hypnosis in a child, always talk to him at his intellectual level. If possible, make the induction procedure a sort of game. Use his imagination to "look" at a TV program. Get him to play a role in it or have him resort to some type of daydreaming fantasies. Imagery techniques are more effective if the ideas are incorporated into the child's imagination. Let him think he controls the situation by having him decide what environment to place himself in.

"You will pay more and more attention to the television screen. Keep looking at it.

"As you are looking at it, you will notice that your right arm will begin to lift up into the air by itself. That's right. It is beginning to lift. It is lifting, lifting, lifting. Higher and higher.

"Just keep looking at the picture. Your arm is lifting still higher. Listen to everything that is said and, as you keep looking at the screen, you are getting *very, very tired*.

"And now your arm is raised straight toward the ceiling. If you wish, you can become more and more deeply relaxed.

"Just say to yourself, think to yourself, 'My arm is getting stiffer and *stiffer*. Rigid!' And, if you wish to go *deeper,* slowly allow your arm to fall, and as it falls you too will go deeper and deeper."

MECHANICAL TECHNIQUES

Any steady, monotonous sound has a tendency to induce relaxation. Any regular sound, such as the ticking of a watch, a metronome, or a clock, the constant falling of drops of water, or even listening to a heartbeat (a stethoscope placed in your ears) will induce hypno-relaxation. Simply suggest that your eyes will be opened and closed alternately with every sound of the watch or beat of the metronome or the heart.

A small microphone can be used to amplify and conduct your own heart and respiratory sounds to your ears. The rhythm of the heartbeat acts as a monotonous fixation stimulus and the monotonic effect of the breath sounds serves as a conditioned stimulus for sleep. A verbalization technique also can be employed with this method. Another variation is to use intermittent visual stimuli, such as is provided by a flashlight, which can go on and off in synchrony with the metronome. Counting backwards or forward is also helpful with either of these techniques.

A rotating mirror or a brightly colored fish lure can accomplish the same effects. All these techniques can be combined with appropriate suggestions for relaxation. There are many other devices, such as hypnodiscs and tape and record players, that can induce some degree of hypnosis in susceptible individuals (see Chapter 5). There is no device, per se, that is 100 per cent effective in inducing hypnosis. Invariably a standard verbalization technique is necessary.

AWAKENING FROM THE TRANCE

"Now, in a few moments … when I count up to five … you will open your eyes and be wide awake again.

"You will feel much better for this deep, refreshing sleep.

"You will feel completely relaxed,…both mentally and physically,… quite calm and composed,…without the slightest feeling of drowsiness or tiredness.

"And, next time … you will not only be able to go into this sleep much more quickly and easily … but you will be able to go much more deeply.

"Each time, in fact … your sleep will become deeper and deeper.

"One … two … three … four … five … wide awake and refreshed."

CHAPTER 7

ADVANCED INDUCTION TECHNIQUES

ERICKSON'S HAND LEVITATION INDUCTION

"I want you to sit comfortably in the chair.

"Let yourself relax.

"Place your hands, palms downward, on your thighs.

"Fix your eyes upon your hands … and keep watching them … very, very closely.

"And while you are relaxing like this,…you will notice that certain things are happening … that you had not noticed before.

"I will point them out to you.

"Now, I want you to concentrate on all the sensations and feelings that you notice in your hands … no matter what they may be.

"It may be that you will feel the texture of the material of your trousers … as your hands rest on your thighs.

"You may feel the warmth of your hand on your leg … or you may feel a certain amount of tingling in your hand.

"No matter what your sensations may be, I want you to observe them closely.

"Keep watching your hand.

"It seems to be quite still ... and resting in one position.

"Yet some movement is there ... although it is not yet noticeable.

"Keep watching your hand.

"Don't let your attention wander from it.

"Just wait to see what movement is going to show itself."

Your attention is now firmly fixed on your hand and you are curious about what is going to happen. Sensations that anyone might normally feel have been suggested to you as possibilities. No attempt has been made to force any suggestion on you. What you observe is a product of your own experience.

A subtle attempt is being made to establish a link in your mind between your own sensations and the words spoken to you. In this way at a later stage this linkage will tend to cause words or commands to produce further sensations or actions.

Unless there is conscious resistance on your part, a slight twitching or jerking will occur in one of your fingers or in your hand. As soon as this happens, your attention must be drawn to the fact that the movement will probably increase. Any other movement of the legs or body, or any alteration in the breathing should also be commented upon. This linking of your reactions with your remarks causes an association between the two to be formed in your mind.

"It will be interesting to see which of your fingers moves first.

"It may be any finger ... or it may even be your thumb.

"But one of the fingers is going to twitch or move.

"You don't know which one ... or even in which hand.

"Neither do I....But keep watching and you will find that one of them will move.

"Possibly in your right hand.

"See! The thumb twitched and moved ... just as I said.

"And now you will notice that a very interesting thing is beginning to happen.

"You will notice that the spaces between your fingers are gradually beginning to widen.

"The fingers will move slowly apart ... and you'll see that the spaces will become wider and wider.

"Your fingers are slowly moving apart … wider … wider … wider.

"The spaces are slowly becoming wider … wider … wider."

(This is the first suggestion you are expected to respond to. If the fingers do move apart, it is because you are beginning to respond to suggestion. The tape continues to talk, however, as if it were something that had taken place in the natural course of events.)

"Now, I want you to watch carefully what is taking place.

"Your fingers will want to rise up slowly from off your thigh.

"As if they want to lift up … higher … higher … higher."

(Your forefinger starts to move upward slightly.

"You see!
"Already your forefinger is beginning to lift up.

"As it does so … all the other fingers will want to follow.

"Up … and up … and up.

"Rising up slowly into the air."

(The other fingers begin to rise.)

"As the other fingers lift … your whole hand is beginning to feel lighter and lighter.

"So light … that your whole hand will slowly rise into the air.

"As if it feels just as light as a feather … just like a feather.

"As if a balloon is slowly lifting it up in the air. Lifting … lifting … up … and up … and up. Pulling it up … higher,…higher,…higher.

"Your hand is becoming lighter and lighter.

"Very, very light indeed."

(The hand starts to rise.)

"As you watch your hand rise … you will feel that your whole arm is beginning to feel lighter and lighter.

"It wants to rise up in the air.

"Notice how your arm is lifting up into the air … up … and up … and up,…a little higher … and higher … and higher."

(Your arm has now lifted about six inches [15 cm] above the thigh, and you are gazing at it intently.)

"Keep watching your hand and arm … as it rises into the air.

"And as it does so … you will begin to feel drowsy and tired.

"Notice how drowsy and tired your eyes are becoming.

"As your arm continues to rise … you will feel more and more tired and relaxed … very, very sleepy,…very, very sleepy indeed.

"Your eyes will become heavier and heavier … and your eyelids will want to close.

"As your arm rises … higher and higher … you will want to feel more and more relaxed.

"You will want to enjoy this very, very pleasant,… relaxed,…sleepy feeling.

"Just let yourself go.

"Give yourself up entirely to this very, very comfortable,… relaxed,…drowsy feeling."

(Notice how as you carry out one suggestion, your response is used to reinforce and facilitate the next suggestion. As your arm rises, it is suggested by inference that you will become drowsy because your arm is rising.)

"Your arm is lifting up … and up … and up.

"Higher … and higher … and higher.

"And you are feeling very, very drowsy indeed.

"Your eyelids are becoming heavier … and heavier.

"Your breathing is becoming slower … and deeper. Breathe slowly and deeply … in … and out … in … and out."

(Your arm is now stretched out straight in front of you. Your eyes are beginning to blink, and your breathing is deep and regular.)

"As you keep watching your hand and arm,…you are feeling more and more drowsy … and relaxed.

"And now you will notice that your hand is changing its direction.

"The elbow is beginning to bend … and your hand is beginning to move … closer and closer to your face.

"Your hand feels as though it were being strongly attracted to your face.

"Your hand is moving … slowly but surely … towards your face.

"And as it comes closer and closer … you are feeling drowsier and drowsier,…and you will fall into a very deep sleep.

"Closer and closer,…drowsier and drowsier … more and more sleepy.

"Although you are becoming more and more sleepy … you must not go to sleep until your hand touches your face.

"But when your hand touches your face … you will fall immediately into a deep, deep sleep."

(You are being asked to choose your own pace in falling asleep, consequently when your hand touches your face and your eyes do close, you are perfectly satisfied that you are, in fact, asleep. Constant coupling of the hand-levitation and sleepiness techniques causes them to continue to reinforce each other.

When you finally close your eyes, you will have entered a trance that you participated in producing. You will be much less likely to deny that you have been in a trance.)

"Your hand is now changing its direction.

"It is moving closer and closer to your face.

"Your eyelids are feeling heavier and heavier.

"You are becoming sleepier … and sleepier … and sleepier."

(Your hand is now approaching your face, and your eyelids are blinking more rapidly.)

"Your eyes are becoming heavier … and heavier.

"Your hand is moving down and down towards your face.

"You are becoming drowsier … and drowsier … more and more tired.

"Your eyes are closing now … closing … closing.

"When your hand touches your face … they will close immediately.

"You will fall into a very, very deep sleep.

"Drowsier … and drowsier,…very, very sleepy,…very, very tired.

"Your eyelids are beginning to feel just as heavy as lead.

"Your hand is moving closer and closer to your face.

"Closer … and closer … closer to your face.

"The moment it touches your face … you will fall into a very, very deep sleep."

(Your hand touches your face, and your eyes close.)

"Go to sleep! Go to sleep! Sleep very, very deeply!

"And as you sleep … you will feel very, very tired … and relaxed.

"Let yourself go.…Let yourself relax completely.

"Think of nothing but sleep,…*deep, deep sleep!"*

You should notice that no attempt whatever is made in the early stages to force any suggestions upon you. Sensations that almost anyone might experience are suggested to you as possibilities. Consequently, as you observe them, you look upon them as a product of your own experience, and this renders you much more likely to respond to them as if they, too, are parts of your own experience.

The first real suggestion is made when you are told that your fingers are beginning to separate. If they do, then you are definitely responding to suggestion. When you are told that as your hand approaches your face you will become drowsier and drowsier, you are actually being requested to choose your own pace in "falling asleep." When your hand eventually touches your face, you will feel yourself to be asleep to your own complete satisfaction, and will then be much less likely to deny the fact that you have been hypnotized.

There is little doubt that when you are hypnotized for the first time by this method, you will usually achieve depth hypnosis much more easily than you would, had any other method of induction been used.

ERICKSON'S CONFUSIONAL TECHNIQUE

The main object of this technique is to set up a situation in which you are never sure whether you are actually cooperating or not, and under these circumstances your defenses become ineffective. When using confusional techniques, your voice on tape must maintain a casual but interested attitude and you must speak seriously and intently, as if you expect to understand exactly what is being said. The tenses must be carefully and constantly shifted, and a ready flow of language maintained. You should be given a little time to respond, but never quite sufficient for you to react fully before the next idea is presented. You consequently become so confused and frustrated that you feel a growing need for a clear-cut communication to which you can respond.

"Your right hand is rising into the air … and your left hand is pressing down on the arm of the chair.

"Let your left hand rise into the air … and your right hand press down on the arm of the chair.

"Both hands are pressing down on the arms of the chair.

"One hand is now lifting up into the air … and the other is pressing down on the arm of the chair.

"Your right hand is rising into the air … and your left hand is pressing down on the arm of the chair…"

(Original suggestion.)

Confused by these rapidly conflicting instructions, in sheer desperation you are likely to accept and carry out the first positive suggestion that will enable you to escape from your dilemma. Please refer to Chapter 11 for a discussion on Erickson.

THE INHIBITION OF VOLUNTARY MOVEMENTS

"I want you to hold your arms straight out in front of you. Hold them as stiff and rigid as you can, and clasp your hands together.

"Lock your fingers together and keep them tightly locked together.

"Tighter and tighter."

(At this point, it is helpful to press your clasped hands firmly together.)

"As you clasp your hands tighter and tighter together … you will feel your fingers gripping more and more firmly.

"And as they do so … I want you to picture a heavy metal vise.

"Imagine you can see the jaws of that vise … being screwed together more and more tightly.

"Now, picture that vise clearly in your mind … and concentrate on it.

"And as you do so … just imagine that your hands represent the jaws of that vise … that they are slowly becoming screwed together … more and more tightly.

"As I count up to *five* … your hands are becoming locked together … more and more tightly … and when I reach the count of *five* … they will be so tightly locked … they will feel just like a solid block of metal … and it will be quite impossible for you to separate them.

"*One* … tightly locked,…*two* … more and more tightly,… *three* … very, very tight,…*four* … the palms of your hands are locked tightly together,…*five* … *they are so tightly locked that it will be impossible for you to separate them until I count to three.…The harder you try to separate the palms of your hands,…the tighter your fingers will press on the back of your hands … and the tighter your hands will become locked together.*"

CHAPTER 8

BASIC DEEPENING TECHNIQUES

❖

DEEPENING IS ACHIEVED by establishing a definite goal for each step of the induction procedure by such phrases as, "As you raise your arm higher and higher, and with every motion of your arm upward, you will go deeper and deeper, becoming more and more relaxed." Linking these suggestions with ongoing physiologic processes is helpful here, too. For example: "With each beat, beat of your heart, you will go deeper and deeper, becoming more and more relaxed."

Deepening can be more effective if words such as "deeper and deeper" and "heavier and heavier" are given to coincide with your actual breathing. You are to follow the procedure as outlined below for practicing autohypnosis, three times a day, five to 10 minutes each time, at home. Practice is very important to obtain proper self-control. By coordinating your body functioning (ideomotor) with thoughts (ideosensory), you can easily develop these deepening techniques.

DEEPENING BY THE RELATION OF DEPTH TO PERFORMANCE
You are repeatedly told to relate the performance of something that is actually happening to you during the hypnotic state to further deepening of the trance. Similarly, any feeling that you are experiencing can be similarly related to an increase in depth.

"As your arm falls limply back on to your lap … you are falling into a deeper, deeper sleep.

"As your hand floats upwards into the air … your sleep is becoming deeper and deeper

"As you feel more and more relaxed … so you are falling into a deeper, deeper sleep."

DEEPENING USING COUNTING AND BREATHING TECHNIQUES

"I am going to count slowly up to *five* … and as I do so … you will take *five very deep breaths*.

"And with each deep breath that you take … each time you breathe out … you will become more and more relaxed … and your sleep will become deeper and deeper.

"*One* … Deep, deep breath … more and more deeply relaxed … more and more deeply asleep.

"*Two* … Very deep breath … more and more deeply relaxed … sleep becoming deeper and deeper.

"*Three* … Deeper and deeper breath … more and more deeply relaxed … more and more deeply asleep.

"*Four* … Very, very deep breath … more and more deeply relaxed … sleep becoming even deeper and deeper.

"*Five* … Very, very deep breath indeed … very, very deeply relaxed … very, very deeply asleep."

DEEPENING BY ARM-LEVITATION

"Let yourself relax completely … and breathe quietly … in … and out.

"And as you do so … you will gradually sink into a deeper, deeper sleep.

"And as you sink into this deeper, deeper sleep … I want you to concentrate on the sensations you can feel in your left hand and arm.

"You will feel that your left hand is gradually becoming lighter and lighter.

"It feels just as though your wrist were tied to a balloon … as if it were gradually being pulled up … higher and higher … away from the chair.

"It wants to rise up … into the air … towards the ceiling.

"Let it rise … higher and higher.

"Just like a cork … floating on water.

"And, as it floats up … into the air … your whole body feels more and more relaxed … heavier and heavier … and you are slowly sinking into a deeper, deeper sleep.

"Your left hand feels even lighter and lighter.

"Rising up into the air … as if it were being pulled up towards the ceiling.

"Lighter and lighter … light as a feather.

"Breathe deeply … and let yourself relax completely.

"And as your hand gets lighter and lighter … and rises higher and higher into the air … your body is feeling heavier and heavier … and you are falling into a deep, deep sleep.

"Now your whole arm, from the shoulder to the wrist, is becoming lighter and lighter.

"It is leaving the chair … and floating upwards … into the air.

"Up it comes … into the air,…higher and higher.

"Let it rise … higher and higher,…higher and higher.

"It is slowly floating up … into the air … and as it does so … you are falling into a deeper, deeper sleep."

FURTHER DEEPENING BY ARM-HEAVINESS

"And now you will feel your arm becoming heavier and heavier again.

"Heavier and heavier,…just like a lead weight.

"It is slowly sinking downwards … onto the chair again.

"Let it go … heavy as lead.…Let it sink down … farther and farther.

"And as it does so … you are falling into an even deeper sleep.

"Deeper and deeper,…more and more deeply asleep.

"Your arm is feeling heavier and heavier,…heavy as lead.

"It is sinking down now … onto the chair.

"And as it does so … you are falling into a deeper, deeper sleep.

"The moment your arm touches the chair … you will be in a very, very deep sleep."

ESCALATOR TECHNIQUE

"Visualize, if you will, that you are in an elevator on a high floor. Notice the number of the floor. Perhaps it is the 16th floor or the 20th floor. Notice the number on the landing. And now the elevator is beginning to descend, and as you feel it *descending,* you, too, will feel yourself descending, *feeling more and more deeply* relaxed. As each number on the landing gets smaller and smaller, you will fall *deeper* and *feel more and more deeply relaxed. Deeper and deeper relaxed.* When the elevator stops at the ground floor, you will be in a *deep, deep state of state of relaxation.* You are in a deep, pleasant, soothing, refreshing state in which you will listen to every suggestion that you wish to follow."

DEEPENING BY PROGRESSIVE RELAXATION

"Now a feeling of complete relaxation is gradually stealing over your whole body.

"Let the muscles of your feet and ankles relax completely.

"Let them go … limp and slack.

"Now, your calf muscles.

"Let them go limp and slack.…Allow them to relax.

"Now, the muscles of your thighs.

"Let them relax.…Let them go … limp and slack.

"And as the muscles of your legs and thighs become completely limp and relaxed,…you can feel a feeling of heaviness in your legs.

"As though your legs are becoming just as heavy as lead.

"Just let your legs go,…heavy as lead.

"Let them relax completely.

"And as your legs do so … your sleep is becoming deeper and deeper.

"That feeling of relaxation is now spreading upwards … over your whole body.

"Let your stomach muscles relax.…Let them go … limp and slack.

"Now, the muscles of your chest,…your body,…and your back.

"Let them all go … limp and slack.…Allow them to relax.

"And as you do so … you can feel a feeling of heaviness in your body … as though your body is becoming just as heavy as lead.

"As if it wanted to sink down … deeper and deeper … into the chair.

"Just let your body go,…heavy as lead.

"Let it sink back comfortably,…deeper and deeper … into the chair.

"And as it does so … you are gradually falling into a deeper, deeper sleep.

"Just give yourself up completely … to this very pleasant,… relaxed, …drowsy feeling.

"And now, this feeling of relaxation is spreading into the muscles of your neck,…your shoulders,…and your arms.

"Let your neck muscles relax,…particularly the muscles at the back of your neck.

"Let them relax.…Let them go … limp and slack.

"Now, your shoulder muscles.

"Let them go limp and slack.…Allow them to relax.

"Now, the muscles of your arms.

"Let them relax.…Let them go limp and slack.

"And as you do so … you can feel a feeling of heaviness in your arms.

"As though your arms are becoming as heavy as lead.

"Let your arms go,…heavy as lead.

"And as you do so … your sleep is becoming deeper,…deeper,…deeper.

"And as this feeling of complete relaxation spreads … and deepens over your whole body … you have fallen into a very, very deep sleep indeed.

"You are so deeply asleep … *that everything I tell you that is going to happen … will happen … exactly as I tell you.*

"And every feeling that I tell you that you will experience … you will experience … exactly as I tell you.

"Now, sleep very, very deeply.

"More and more deely asleep.…More and more deeply asleep."

CHAPTER 9

ADVANCED DEEPENING TECHNIQUES

❖

VOGT'S FRACTIONATION TECHNIQUE

Before dehypnotization, the subject working with a hypnotist is asked to relate the thoughts, feelings and sensations he experienced at the moment of his maximal relaxation. The individual is then dehypnotized. These sensations are fed back when rehypnotized. He is told that he will go deeper with each rehypnotization. For instance, if he states, "I felt I was floating on fleecy white clouds," incorporate this into the next induction procedure by stating, "You will go deeper and deeper as you feel yourself floating on fleecy white clouds." If he remarks, "I saw all kinds of colored flashes of light," tell him, "Now, as soon as you see these colored flashes, you will relax more and more deeply." The elicited subjective information is repetitively utilized for immediately deepening each phase of the induction until a deep state is attained. Vogt's fractionation technique simply depends on the subject's being dehypnotized, questioned and then reinduced by feeding in those relaxing sensations which he has just described. This procedure is repeated again and again until a deep state of relaxation is achieved.

For self-hypnosis, simply play a tape of this script and follow along with the instructions as best as you can.

"I am now going to awaken you by counting up to five.

"After I have done so ... although your eyes will be open ... while I

66

am talking to you,…you will begin to feel very, very drowsy and sleepy again.

"You will find it harder and harder to keep your eyes open … and to stay awake.

"Your eyes will feel very, very heavy.…The eyelids will feel heavier and heavier … and will begin to blink.

"You will not be able to stop them blinking.

"And as they blink,…you will find it more and more difficult to keep them open.

"They will want to close.…You will not be able to stop them from closing.

"Every moment … as I go on talking … you will feel drowsier and drowsier … sleepier and sleepier.

"Your eyes will close … and you will fall into a deep, deep sleep.

"You will be in a much deeper sleep than you are now!

"I am going to count slowly up to five.

"As I do so … you will open your eyes and wake up.

"But you will feel very, very drowsy … very, very sleepy.

"Your eyes will feel so heavy … so very, very tired … that you will not be able to keep them open for long.

"They will start to blink … you will be unable to stop them from blinking.

"And as they do so … your eyes will feel so very, very tired that they will close … and you will fall into a much, much deeper sleep!"

(After being awakened, your eyes will either start to blink, or they may seem to remain sleepy and half-closed. This must be followed up immediately:)

"You see! Your eyes are feeling heavier and heavier!

"You are feeling very, very drowsy … and sleepy.

"Your eyes are closing … and you are falling into a deeper, deeper sleep."

(Sometimes, this will be unnecessary since the eyes will not only start to blink but will also close entirely on their own. In this case, the above suggestions should be modified accordingly.)

"You see! Your eyes *have* closed on their own.

"Sleep very, very deeply ... very, very deeply.

"More and more deeply asleep,...more and more deeply asleep!"

DEEPENING BY THE DISSOCIATION METHOD

This depends on the production in your mind of a fantasy that you are actually watching someone else being induced into a deep hypnotic state. Since you begin by "dissociating" yourself from what is taking place, your own resistance is not aroused. The description of what is occurring, however, gradually induces you to identify yourself with the supposed subject, and you begin to feel that the phenomena are actually happening to you. You are able to allow this to happen because your resistance never becomes activated.

"I want you to imagine that you are standing outside a consulting-room door.

"You are beginning to feel quite strange ... and as you grasp the handle of the door ... and slowly open it ... this feeling of strangeness is increasing.

"As you walk into the room ... you feel as though you are a complete stranger.

"There is a doctor in the room, who is dealing with a patient.

"The doctor is wearing..."

(Here you describe roughly what you, the doctor, are wearing.)

"The patient is wearing..."

(Here you describe what your patient is actually wearing.)

"Now, watch the doctor [you] ... and notice what is happening to the patient with him.

"He is talking to the patient ... and as he does so ... something very curious is happening.

"See how the patient's right hand and arm are starting to float up into the air.

"His right hand is floating up,...and up,...and up. Now, his whole arm is floating up,...and up,...and up.

"And as it does so,...you can see that he is falling into a deeper, deeper sleep."

(During this description, your own arm usually starts to rise as you identify yourself with the patient.)

THE IDEOMOTOR FINGER-SIGNALING TECHNIQUE

When you prepare your mind for the acceptance of hypnosis, you can learn how to pay attention to some part of the body, and not to pay attention to another. You can be trained to relax your muscles. You can also learn how muscles can react "subconsciously," and thus establish a method of communication at a subconscious level by using the subconscious movements of the finger-muscles to indicate the answers "yes," "no," or "I don't want to answer" to the questions that you put to yourself.. I have found the following approach to be most effective:

"I want you to put both hands on your lap … and I'll show you how you can learn to answer questions at a subconscious level.

"When you are talking to people … you have often seen them nod their heads when they agree with you … and shake their heads when they disagree with what you are saying.

"And they don't even know they are doing so.

"The movement is completely subconscious.

"Now,…I'm going to teach your subconscious mind how it can answer questions by causing one finger to rise for the answer yes, and a different one for the answer no.

"Just let your hands lie idly upon your lap.

"I want you to think the thought … *yes,….yes,…yes,*…over and over again.

"And as you do so … you will soon feel one of your fingers beginning to lift up on its own … from your lap.

"It's just like getting a swing going … you have to keep pushing it at intervals.

"You do this by thinking … *yes* over and over.

"And while you keep on thinking … *yes* … you are not thinking *no* … or any other answer.

"Just keep on thinking … *yes* … *yes* … *yes*.

"There … you see.

"The forefinger of your right hand is slowly lifting up.

"Put it down again.

"Now ... think the thought ... *no,...no,...no,*...over and over again.

"And ... as you do so ... one of your other fingers will slowly rise.

"It may be on the same hand ... or it may be on the other hand.

"There you are.

"It's the forefinger of your *left* hand.

"So ... if I ask your subconscious mind a question ... and the answer is *yes,* ....after it has considered the question ... it will cause your right forefinger to rise.

"If,...on the other hand,...the answer is *no* ... your left forefinger will rise."

(A third finger may, of course, be conditioned to signify the response "*I would prefer not to answer,*" should this be considered desirable.)

"Now ... I'm going to ask your subconscious mind one or two questions.

"Your conscious mind doesn't know the real cause of your illness.

"Neither does mine.

"But your own *subconscious* mind does.

"And it can help you ... in this way ... to get to the real root of your trouble.

"Is your unconscious mind ready to help?"

(The right forefinger slowly rises.... *Yes.*)

"Does it object to being questioned in this way?"

(The *left* forefinger slowly rises....*No.*)

At this time you can now ask your subconscious mind for the reason for your block towards deepening the trance. Ideomotor signaling can be of distinct advantage when you want to explore something that has been repressed for a long time.

CHAPTER 10

OVERCOMING RESISTANCE

❖

WHENEVER DIFFICULTY OCCURS, it is most important to try to discover the nature of the difficulty you are confronted with. It may be that the technique you have adopted will have to be modified to suit your needs, but even this cannot properly be decided until the nature of the difficulty is known. The best way of approaching this problem is to question yourself closely as to the precise sensations you experienced during the induction, and any difficulties that you may have felt.

The most common causes of resistance to hypnosis are:

1. Over-anxiety and fear of failure

2. Fear of the hypnotic state itself

3. Inadequate preparation before induction

4. Fluctuating attention

5. Physical discomfort

6. Dislike of the method of induction employed

7. Lack of motivation

1. Over-anxiety and fear of failure
This is a very common source of difficulty. Indeed, over-anxiety to succeed with hypnosis is almost bound to interfere with successful induction.

71

The only way of dealing with this situation is to give yourself the strongest possible reassurance and encouragement before proceeding with any further attempts at induction.

2. Fear of the hypnotic state itself

It sometimes happens that while you may be consciously anxious and willing to be hypnotized, you may also be subconsciously afraid of succumbing to the trance. When this is so, your subconscious fear is usually that of "losing control," and the mental conflict that consequently arises is quite sufficient to prevent you from entering the hypnotic state at all.

3. Inadequate preparation before induction

Most of the difficulties encountered in trance induction will be greatly lessened, if not entirely removed, if your mind has been fully prepared before any attempt is made. A review of Chapter 4 on the pre-induction discussion will illustrate a proper preparation for hypnosis.

4. Fluctuating attention

This usually occurs when one has what is aptly called a "grasshopper" mind. This refers to your powers of concentration, and a mind that cannot remain fixed on one idea or hold attention long enough to permit the induction to become successful. It flits incessantly from one topic to another.

The best way of dealing with this, by far, is to use a modified counting technique. The following modification is the one I have found to be most satisfactory:

> "I want you to start counting slowly to yourself ... and to go on counting until you hear me tell you to stop.
>
> "When you say...'*one,*'...close your eyes!
>
> "When you say...'*two,*'...open your eyes!
>
> "When you say...'*three,*'...close your eyes!
>
> "When you say...'*four,*'...open your eyes."
>
> (As you count to yourself, open and shut your eyes deliberately with each alternate count. While you are doing this, quietly tell yourself how sleepy you are becoming, that your eyes are becoming more and more tired and your eyelids heavier and heavier, that presently they will want to remain closed and you will fall into a deep, deep sleep.)

5. Physical discomfort

Physical discomfort can greatly hinder the successful induction of hypnosis, therefore you should always be made as comfortable as possible. Make sure to use the bathroom before settling down on the couch or chair. Drafts should be avoided, and you should keep warm. Loud and unexpected noises should be avoided if possible.

6. Dislike of the method of induction employed

Sometimes you may dislike the method of induction or you may dislike something in the actual phrasing of your own suggestions. For instance, you might object to the word *sleepy*. If so, you should discard it completely and substitute the words *tiredness* and *drowsiness* only, during the next induction. Similarly, when the phrase *you are sinking into a deeper, deeper sleep* has been used, you might complain that upon the word "sinking" you invariably experienced a most uncomfortable sinking sensation in the pit of your stomach. In this case, the mere substitution of the word "falling" will be quite sufficient to remove this discomfort. Whenever it is the actual induction method that you dislike, you should always adopt an alternative procedure at your next attempt at induction.

7. Lack of motivation

If you have little or no desire to get well, you are going to be a poor subject for hypnosis. It is almost impossible to induce hypnosis unless you are sufficiently motivated. Many people, such as alcoholics, smokers, and overeaters, do not wish to yield their symptoms because they have a "self-defeating sequence" mentality. These "self-defeating sequences" or self-sabotage can be removed by raising the individual's self-image (which, in reality, is the alpha level). Motivation is the single most important factor in the ability to experience hypnosis.

CHAPTER 11

BEHAVIOR MODIFICATION
THROUGH HYPNOSIS

❖

JOSEPH WOLPE DEVELOPED A method known as the reciprocal inhibition principle for the treatment of habits and phobias. His 90 percent "apparently cured" and "much improved" rates have been positively evaluated by thousands of studies. He contends that a habit can be eradicated by forming a new and antagonistic one toward the same stimulus situation. By deliberately opposing responses antagonistic to anxiety responses, neurotic anxiety response habits can be overcome.

Since neurotic behavior originates in learning, it can be eliminated only by "unlearning." In utilizing a systematic desensitization approach, phobias can be easily treated. While in hypnosis the patient is given suggestions to expose himself gradually to the terrifying situation. The aim in desensitization is to get the patient to master his fears by actually facing them. It is essential for the individual to force himself again and again into the phobic situation, in order to learn to control it.

For example, if a person fears open spaces or going outdoors, on the first day he can walk several steps from his house and then return. On the second day he can increase the distance between himself and his house, and so on, until he is able to walk a considerable distance from his home. The hope is that the conquering of graduated doses of his fear will desensitize him to its influence. This is accomplished by the construction of hierarchies.

The hierarchy construction is emphasized to be of the greatest importance, since the systematic desensitization procedure is focused on the individual hierarchically arranged items. Histories, questionnaires, and fear surveys are often used to derive the hierarchy material. Wolpe places the stimulus with the greatest anxiety-producing value at the top. The remaining stimuli are ranked in order downwards. Each anxiety or phobic hierarchy has its own separate theme, and specific stimuli are ranked according to the amount of anxiety they evoke.

The desensitization process begins once relaxation training appears sufficient and hierarchy construction is complete. To begin the process, you relax yourself and then ask yourself to visualize an anxiety-producing item from the lower end of the hierarchy. Since the item was only minimally anxiety-producing initially, its visualization in the context of the relaxation weakens its anxiety-producing value still further. By arousing a mildly anxiety-producing stimulus antagonistic to anxiety, the counter-conditioning of that anxiety response (relaxation) results. Upon repetition, it is eliminated.

The next item in the hierarchy is then presented, and relaxation is re-emphasized. This is continued on up the hierarchy until all stimuli have been desensitized. At any time during the procedure you can signal excessive anxiety feelings by raising a finger. In such an instance, simply return to relaxation instructions before repeating the stimulus visualization.

For example, the following hierarchy was constructed by a patient with a fear of flying:

1. A light-headed feeling from the plane's motion
2. The pilot announces a delay in landing
3. Looking at my watch and noticing we should have landed at this time
4. The "No smoking; fasten seat belt" signs go on at an unexpected time
5. Turbulence
6. Reduction or changes in engine sounds
7. Overhearing a passenger talk about an airliner crash
8. Changes in the cabin lighting
9. Feeling of being pushed back in seat as the plane goes down the runway for take-off
10. The first part of the take-off when I look outside
11. Getting ready for take-off, the doors slam shut

12. Taxiing for take-off

13. Walking up the stairway to going down ramp to board the aircraft

14. Standing in line to check bags

15. Buying the tickets in advance

16. The morning of the trip

17. The night before the trip

18. Two days before the trip

19. Five days before the trip

20. A week before the trip

21. At home or in the office realizing, This is it—the trip by plane can't be avoided

22. Watching an airplane take off on television

Once you have entered a relaxed state, you then introduce the first imagery scene from the hierarchy.

> *"As you continue to relax like that, automatically going deeper and deeper, I want you to picture yourself relaxing at home in your favorite chair, just watching TV, relaxing more and more all the time. You're watching TV and the program shows an airplane taking off.*

> (Pause for three seconds.)

> *"Just switch off that image now and go back to relaxing."*

The anxiety-producing value of this scene will often be reduced to virtually zero after about four presentations, provided the hierarchy was quantified on a physiological basis. Once the zero or near-zero arousal level has been reached, you may proceed to the next item. If a maximum of about 15 minutes beyond the initial relaxation period is devoted to the actual desensitization, your time to the zero arousal criterion will determine this factor. Early sessions may involve only one or two items, while later sessions often involve as many as 20.

> *"As you continue to relax like that, you find you can relax more and more. You notice that you are becoming less anxious—more relaxed—with each scene. Now I want you to imagine it's one week before the trip when you must fly in an airplane; just picture that in your mind. Now just switch that scene off, letting yourself become more and more relaxed all over. You can relax more and more on your own, enjoying the ability to control your own level of relaxation. Good. That's fine. Relaxing more and more, easing up, feeling calm and serene. The*

next time I give you the scene, just as in real life, your anxiety level will be much, much lower; you will be able to relax throughout the visualization. Now once again, just imagine it's one week before the trip on when you must fly in an airplane."

DENTAL PHOBIA HIERARCHY

For a dental phobia, one of my dental patients prepared the following hierarchy:

1. Having a tooth removed

2. Having a root canal performed

3. Having a dental impression

4. Having dental instruments manipulated in your mouth

5. Having a tooth drilled and worked on

6. Receiving the anesthetic injection

7. Seeing the needles and syringe

8. Having a probe placed in a cavity

9. Seeing the dental instruments

10. Hearing the noise of the drill

11. The dentist tells you that you have many dental problems

12. Having the dentist squirt air and water in your mouth

13. Having your teeth cleaned

14. Having dental x-rays taken

15. The dentist walks into the treatment room

16. Reclining in a dental chair

17. Sitting up in a dental chair

18. Smelling the smell of a dentist's office

19. Sitting in the dentist's waiting room

20. Calling to make a dental appointment

21. Thinking about going to the dentist

Common sense, diligence, and proper motivation make this an excellent approach to removing simple habits and phobias, following any standard hypnotic induction.

CHAPTER 12

ERICKSONIAN HYPNOSIS

I HAVE INTRODUCED some of the late Milton Erickson's induction techniques in Chapter 6. Erickson's contribution represents an important shift away from the authoritarian methods of the past to his pioneering work with the more permissive and insightful approaches characteristic of our current era. It is now recognized that the most significant person in the hypnotherapeutic interaction is the patient, not the therapist. The patient's potential accounts for most of what actually happens in hypnotherapy, not the purported "powers" of the hypnotist. The therapist does not command the patient; rather, Erickson noted, "It is always a matter of offering them [patients] the opportunity of responding to an idea." It is now recognized that the hypnotherapist offers the patient many approaches to hypnotic experience rather than imposing hypnotic techniques.

The concept of technique implies the mechanical and repetitious application of a particular procedure in the same way to every patient with the intent of producing a preconceived and predictable response. The concept of approaches implies alternatives to help each patient bypass his or her own particular learned limitations so that the various hypnotic phenomena and hypnotherapeutic responses may be experienced.

Erickson stated his basic philosophy to hypnotherapy as follows:

"I like to regard my patients as having a conscious mind and an unconscious, or subconscious, mind. I expect the two of them to be together in the same person, and I expect both of them to be in the office with me. *When I am talking to a person at the conscious level, I expect him to be listening to me at an unconscious level, as well as consciously.* And therefore I am not very greatly concerned about the depth of the trance the patient is in because I find that one can do extensive and deep psychotherapy in the light trance as well as in the deeper medium trance. One merely needs to know how to talk to a patient in order to secure therapeutic results."

Erickson disliked all forms of authoritarian techniques. He stated:

"I do not like this matter of telling a patient, 'I want you to get tired and sleepy, and to get tired and sleepier.' That is an effort to force your wishes upon the patient. That is an effort to dominate the patient. It is much better to suggest that they *can* get tired, that they can get sleepy, that they can go into a trance. For it is always a matter of *offering them the opportunity of responding to an idea.*"

METALEVELS

Erickson emphasized that the therapist is always working with a frame of reference rather than the actual words. In hypnotherapy, when you are talking to a patient, you are actually addressing his frame of reference. You are using his own words to alter the patient's access to his various frames of reference. That's the therapeutic response: gaining access to a new frame of reference.

A patient is a patient because he does not know how to use his different frames of reference in a skillful manner. Erickson believed these frames of reference are actually metalevels of communication. Metacommunication is communication (on a higher or secondary level) about communication (on a lower or primary level). The metalevels are usually subconscious. You are always dealing with these subconscious metalevels of communication, since they are the determiners of meaning on the primary level in consciousness. Psychological problems have their origin in the limitations of a consciousness that is restricted to one primary level of functioning.

With indirect hypnotic approaches, Erickson dealt with structure on these metalevels rather than the primary level of conscious experience. Patients usually do not know what you are doing because they are limited by the nature of consciousness to the contents of their primary levels of awareness.

Alternatively, these metalevels may actually be right-hemispheric styles of coping that have a peculiar nonrational form of life experience that has been intuitively recognized as healing. In this case, it's necessary to develop a right-hemispheric science of what in the past has been the domain of mysticism, art, and the spiritual modes of healing. For a detailed discussion of this, I refer you to my book, *Soul Healing*.

According to Erickson, there must be an integration of subconscious learning with conscious learning. You can resolve a conflict, a phobia, or an anxiety in the trance state. But unless you do something about it in the waking state, the patient is still likely to have that anxiety or phobia.

Erickson felt that each patient should be treated by an approach custom-designed to that person's issues and personality. He proposed a three-state paradigm:

1. How can a particular patient's own mental mechanisms and habitual associative processes be utilized to create a method of hypnotic induction that is uniquely suitable for that patient?

2. How can the patient's own mental mechanisms and associative processes be utilized to facilitate an experience of all the classical hypnotic phenomena?

3. Now, utilize this background of hypnotic training to help the patient find a uniquely suitable resolution of the presenting problem.

For example, during a hypnotic induction, catalepsy can usually be achieved indirectly by handing the subject an article such as a book and then withdrawing it with a distracting remark when the subject reaches to take it. The subject's arm will remain momentarily suspended in a cataleptic position, as if still awaiting the book. During that precise moment, when arm and hand are suspended, the patient's mind is also suspended and open; this momentary gap in awareness can be filled by any appropriate suggestion offered by the therapist at that precise moment. The patient at that moment of inquiry—"What does he want my hand to do?"—is completely ready to accept whatever idea is presented to him. Hypnosis doesn't come from mere repetition. It comes from facilitating the patient's ability to accept an idea and to respond to that idea.

Erickson's approaches to catalepsy are designed to secure a patient's attention, to focus that attention inward, and to arouse an attitude of wondering or expectancy for further suggestion. Catalepsy is thus an ideal approach for inducing trance and assessing a patient's receptivity. It can be utilized as a basic foundation on which other hypnotic phenomena may be structured.

When the patient's full attention is centered on the stimuli of a well-balanced muscle tone characteristic of catalepsy, the patient tends to experience an analgesia or anesthesia for other sensations or pain in the body. These associations encourage the patient on a conscious level while providing the subconscious with appropriate cues about how the response may be made and actually activating the relevant response sets that can facilitate the appropriate behavioral response.

SYMPTOM SUBSTITUTION

Erickson intentionally manipulates neurotic symptoms in certain people. In these people, direct symptom removal by hypnosis fails and usually results in resistance to further therapy; the neurotic manifestations are maintained continuously until satisfactory adjustments are achieved.

For example, think of a patient who desperately needs to keep his neurotic disability. Since the underlying maladjustments are impossible to correct, Erickson would substitute another neurotic disability similar to the existing one, but non-incapacitating in character. Shifting attention from anxiety-provoking symptoms to less urgent problems makes the patient less preoccupied with his present difficulties. The substitutive symptom also satisfies the personality needs and, as a result, a healthy adjustment to reality occurs. Erickson concludes: "Regardless of how farcical, the above technique met his symptomatic needs."

Symptom-substitution should be used to "trade down" to a less handicapping symptom; the new substitute symptom is more readily removed. The poorly motivated individual, the "psychiatric veteran," or the geriatric patient responds well to symptom-substitution; fortunately, deep hypnosis is seldom required.

Autohypnosis and sensory-imagery conditioning (see Chapter 12) can be combined with symptom-substitution. A more effective response to suggestions occurs during autohypnosis, and this in turn depends on the effort that the patient puts forth and how often and how well he practices. However, the therapist must never go out on a limb by raising the patient's hopes too high. Active participation in meditation, self-reflection, self-absorption (or whatever term is used to indicate that thoughts are subjectively turned inward) must be encouraged in all patients, especially in those who dislike being helped by another person. This approach works well in the patient who has an inordinate need for attention-getting symptoms.

CHAPTER 13

VISUALIZATION TECHNIQUES

❖

THE VISUALIZATION TECHNIQUE itself is so simple that at first it seems improbable that such dramatic results could come from such a deceptively simple procedure. First, you are taught a simplified form of self-hypnosis with a focus on breathing. You are instructed to repeat the word "relax" silently to yourself and to let go of tension in various muscles by focusing on them one at a time. When a state of relaxation has been established, simply visualize a pleasant, natural scene, such as a small brook in a meadow or whatever occurs to you. Enjoy the scene and begin to experience the calming effect both of the fantasy and of holding it in the mind.

These various visualizations act to train the mind. We have already seen how they can be used in hypnotic induction and deepening techniques. Once you master this technique, you can create your own "mental movies" to remove habits and phobias from your psyche.

The following scenes should be practiced to train your subconscious to utilize your subconscious to create impressions suggestive of relaxation and peace.

BLUEBIRD SCENE
You are sitting on the bank of a river looking up at a bluebird perched on the branch of a tree. It is spring. Smell the freshness in the air. Now the bird has left his perch and is starting to fly toward you.

Hear the babbling of the river as the water rushes over the rocks. The bird is drawing closer. Look up the river. At its head you see a pink castle with flags waving from the turrets.

The bird is getting still closer. A breeze blows from out of the woods, bringing to your nostrils the fragrant smells from a picnic lunch that is spread before you on a checkered cloth. There is ham, French bread, cheese, and wine. Notice the pattern of the red and white checks in the spread.

You feel a feather brush against your hand, tickling your skin. Now you feel the weight and heat of the bird as it lights in your hand. You look into the eyes of the bird. You see in his eyes the reflection of you sitting under a tree by a river. You are surrounded by patches of white and yellow daisies. The tree becomes transparent, turns to glass. Hanging from its branches are long strands of a glittering mosslike substance. The bird closes his eyes. The scene is gone.

GARDEN SCENE

You are in the middle of a vast garden. It is midnight. It is midsummer. The air is warm and balmy. The garden stretches for miles and miles.

You are walking down a path. On either side are orange trees. The moon is full and yellow. The orange trees are deep green with brilliant orange oranges, phosphorescent in the moonlight. Oranges are on the ground. They are very ripe. The smell of orange is heavy in the air.

You reach up and pick an orange from the branch. Bite into the orange. The sweet orange juice squirts into your mouth, running down your throat and into your stomach. Taste the orange.

Now you continue walking until you come to a place where two paths cross. Turn right and walk down a path with lemon trees on either side. They are bright yellow in the moonlight. You pick a lemon. Feel the rough outer texture of the lemon peel. You peel the lemon. Smell the lemony fragrance of the lemon rind.

You sink your teeth into the lemon. The sour lemon juice squirts into your mouth. Taste the lemon. Feel saliva flow in your mouth. Your mouth puckers as you swallow the sour lemon juice. You continue walking, the taste and smell of lemon lingering with you.

Suddenly before you is a long, descending, white marble staircase. Dazzling white in the moonlight. You begin to descend the stairs. With every step downward you become more and more deeply relaxed.

When you reach the base of the stairs you will be in a profound state of relaxation....

You are now standing at the base of the stairs. In front of you is a huge marble swimming pool. All around the pool are red and white and yellow roses, velvety soft in the moonlight, covered with dew. The smell of roses is heavy in the air. You take off your clothes. You glide into the pool. The pool is filled with billions of rose petals. You float on your back in the rosewater, looking up at the stars, buoyant in the water.

Now you get out of the water. You stand up. The cool night air touches your wet body. It sends chills down your spine. You are shivering. Goose flesh appears.

Suddenly you smell smoke. You look in the direction the smell is coming from. There is a wooded area on the other side of the pool. You walk over toward the forest, the smell of smoke growing ever stronger in intensity as you approach the wooded area. You walk into the forest. There before you is a blazing bonfire of burning leaves. It smells like autumn. You lie down beside the fire in a bed of dry leaves, the smell of wet earth beneath you, the smell of burning leaves beside you, the starry sky above you. You drift, you float, you dream ... that midsummer's night.

LAKE SCENE

You are walking barefoot down a gravel road. It is mid-June. It is very warm. You are walking down to the lake. On your right is a thatched-roof cottage with a white picket fence around it. Inside is a small garden with cucumbers, tomatoes, carrots, radishes, and lettuce growing.

Beside the garden is an incinerator, burning paper. Particles of light, hot, paper ash are blowing in the wind. They brush against your skin. They are warm and light and ticklish against your flesh.

Now you come to a long flight of stone steps leading down a steep bank to the shoreline. You begin descending the steps. They are cool and moist beneath your feet. There is a cool metal railing of pipe. The bank is forested. There are wildflowers growing–lupines, columbines, and tiger lilies.

You reach the base of the steps, and before you is a wooden dock and a boat house. A dock boy comes out of the boat house. He is loading a white, wooden boat that is tied to the dock. He brings cushions and oars. You get into the boat. Feel it rock beneath the pressure of your body.

The dock boy brings a large red jerrican, which he places on the dock. He hands you the jerrican. He loads the motor and takes the can from you, placing it in the bottom of the boat. The boat is untied and pushed away with an oar.

The dock boy starts the motor. Hear the roar of the engine. The boat speeds out into the lake. The water is like glass. Your hair is blowing from the wind created by the motion of the boat. Feel the cold, light spray against your face. It is exhilarating!

You reach the other side of the lake, where there are tall rushes growing over eight feet (2.5 m) high. The motor is shut off and you begin to row through the channels of water in the rushes. Feel the pulling in your muscles as you dip and pull the oars. Hear the reeds pressing against the boat.

You come to a small clearing in the rushes. The boat is anchored. You lie in the bottom of the boat, gently rocking back and forth, to and fro, by the motion of the ripples on the water. The summer sun makes you feel so lazy. You drift here for hours.

Now it's time to go back. The dock boy pulls up the anchor. He starts the motor and takes the anchor from you, placing it in the bottom of the boat. The boat speeds out of the rushes and heads straight for the opposite shore and the dock. The boat approaches shore, the motor is turned off, and it is docked. You get out of the boat, walk down the dock, up the cool stone steps, and back down the gravel road, going home.

SHANGRI-LA SCENE

You are in a vast meadow with a huge expanse of blue sky above you. It is early spring. Smell the freshness in the air. In the distance you can see snow-covered mountains like the Alps or Himalayas. The meadow is green and covered with white daisies and other wildflowers.

You wish to scale the mountaintops. You take an air pump and place the rubber hose in your mouth. You begin pumping your body with air, filling up like a balloon. The light, dry air inside your body gives you a sensation of weightlessness.

You begin to float up into the blue sky. You are approaching the mountain peaks. It is getting colder as the altitude increases. The cold causes the air inside you to contract. You begin to descend, landing on the ridge of the mountain. It is freezing cold. The wind is blowing bitterly. With your back to the sheer side of the mountain, you inch your way along the ledge, snow blowing in your face.

You come to a pass. On the other side of the pass is another world. You cross the threshold and find yourself in an orchard of peaches. It is warm, like summer. There are fountains and marble statues. Passing through the orchard, you come to a long flight of stone stairs leading to a rock palace.

You walk up the steps and into the temple, finding yourself in a large stone chamber. There before you is a teak table on which is a stack of piping hot pancakes covered with butter and syrup. Next to them is a pitcher of milk. You begin eating the pancakes, washing them down with the milk. You are starved! They taste delicious, and you eat and eat, shoveling the food down.

Suddenly a gong rings. It echoes throughout the chamber. A sliding stone panel opens and an ancient man with a long white beard enters, bearing a frothing glass of pink liquid. It is an ancient yeast drink, a health-food drink. He gives it to you and you drink. The yeast inside your stomach makes you feel lighter and lighter. The light, wet bubbles inside you make you feel airy as a feather. You float along the stone floor as if there were no gravity.

You glide along the floor, out the temple arch, down the steps, and to a river. You float like an inner tube in the river to the very point where you entered the orchard. You are once again at the pass.

Now that you have mastered these exercises, the following visualization techniques require you to utilize your subconscious mind to create mental movies to resolve problems.

HEADACHES

You are lying relaxed on a beach. You can feel the warmth of the sun. As you turn over, your hand touches the hot sand. Feel the heat penetrating the fingers of both of your hands.

Now, a block of ice is gently placed on the top of your head. Feel the cold sensation. The combination of the cold, numb feeling on the top of your head, along with the hot feeling in your fingers makes it physically impossible for you to feel a discomfort in your head.

WEIGHT REDUCTION

Imagine yourself at your ideal weight. See a friend/mate shopping with you. Your friend is amazed at your thin appearance. Now visualize two tables in front of you. One table on the right has all the foods you like that add unwanted weight. List examples of these foods. Now draw a large red "X" through the table and imagine looking at yourself in a sideshow mirror (one that makes you look very wide and short).

The table on the left contains food that is healthy and will not add unwanted weight–fish, tuna, eggs, and lean meat, for example. Now draw a large yellow check mark through the table and imagine looking at yourself in a mirror that makes you appear tall and thin. Mentally tell yourself that you desire only the foods on the check-marked table. Imagine your friends, family, and parents telling you how great you look by *(specify a date)*, weighing only *(specify an amount)*.

Visualize a photograph of yourself at your ideal weight. Visualize a photograph of yourself at your present weight. Now focus on the photograph of yourself at your ideal weight. The other photograph disappears. Imagine how it will feel at your ideal weight, to bend over to tie your shoelace, walk, jog, or wear a bathing suit on the beach.

Now, mentally select an ideal diet that will help you reach your ideal weight. Tell yourself that this is all the food your body will need or desire and it will *not* send hunger pangs for more.

SMOKING

Take a moment now and imagine yourself driving on a road and arriving at a fork in this road. The left fork is a clean, newly paved, unobstructed road leading to a brand new highway. It is labeled for nonsmokers. The right fork is a dirty, rocky, old, obstructed road and leads to a dead end. It is labeled for smokers.

Choose the road you want to take.

CHAPTER 14

A SELF-HYPNOSIS EXERCISE

❖

THE FOLLOWING IS an exercise that I developed in my early years in private practice and comes from one of my office brochures.

Hypnosis is a subject of rich interest to nearly everyone. The fascination it holds is its promise to open to a person a world of rich treasures and self-improvement as if by magic. And nearly everyone at some time or another has a desire or need for self-improvement. Hypnosis seems to be the answer. After all, the hypnotist has the power to make people do things. Doesn't he?

The hypnotist has no power and never did, just skill. Skilled hypnotists in the past were professional entertainers. They deliberately tried to give the false impression that they had a "remarkable power" over the subject and could force him to do things. The power behind hypnosis lies with the subject and his mind. Charged and unleashed, he is free to release all his mental creative power and bring it to bear with amazing results. The capacity of the human mind to solve and create is amazing and remarkable. Self-hypnosis and hypnotic techniques are a way to successfully reach and put to use more of one's own mind.

Genuine and legitimate improvements in oneself are never simple and easy. They require persistence and determination; without them failure will follow.

Hypnosis is pleasant. It is a state of deep concentration. Your conscious mind, however, is relatively weak. It vacillates continuously and will create an endless round of excuses why you should not bother getting something done. It lacks the kind of stabilizing force that the subconscious possesses.

The subconscious mind can best be influenced when one is in a passive or relaxed state, such as in hypnosis. You need to see that this restful quieting of the mind acts to cleanse it, opening it to pure and more elevated thoughts. Hypnosis is going to build both mental vigor and enthusiasm because it removes all the negative fears and thoughts that act as roadblocks to energy, inspiration, and accomplishment. You want to turn your wishes, ideas, or hopes into reality or they remain meaningless to you. The subconscious is the best place to start the undertaking.

I suggest, therefore, that two periods a day be put aside for the purpose of training your subconscious mind. The periods need be only for ten minutes. The best time is very early in the morning shortly after awakening. The other period can be at your convenience during the day, except do not practice it before bedtime unless you are having difficulty in falling asleep.

STAGE 1: Go into a room and close the door to shut out distracting sounds. Lie down on a bed or couch and relax as well as you can for two to five minutes. The mind and body both will tend to relax as you lie inert, and this passive state will open a door that swings its way to the subconscious mind. As you lie quietly, close your eyes and think of a warm, relaxing feeling.

1. Focus all your attention on the muscles in the toes of both of your feet. Imagine this warm, relaxing feeling spreading and surrounding the muscles of the toes of both feet, moving to the backs of both feet and to the heels and ankles. Now imagine this warm feeling moving up the calf muscles of both legs to the kneecap and into the thigh muscles, meeting at the hip bone.

2. The warm, relaxing feeling is moving up the backbone to the middle of your back, surrounding the shoulder blades, and moving into the back of the neck.

3. The warm, relaxing feeling is now moving into the fingers of both hands, just as it did with the toes. This feeling now spreads into the backs of both hands, into the palms, wrists, forearms, elbows, shoulders, and neck, relaxing each and every muscle along its path.

4. The warm, relaxing feeling now moves into the intestines, stomach, chest, and neck muscles.

5. This warm, relaxing feeling moves into the back of the head, the scalp and all the way to the forehead. Now, the facial muscles are relaxed; now the eyes (which are closed), bridge of the nose, jaws (the teeth are separated), chin, ear lobes, and neck. Now each and every muscle in the entire body is completely relaxed.

When you actually develop a generalized relaxed feeling throughout your body or a heaviness in your arms or legs, you have finally reached the stage of light hypnosis. Continue with the exercise for several days, then progress to the second stage which is more advanced. The instructions are made a part of the mental dialogue that you will be thinking to yourself. Read it over two or three times and commit the general idea rather than trying to remember it word-for-word.

STAGE 2: To go deeper into hypnosis is the aim at this time. This can be accomplished in a number of ways. One of the more common is to imagine a very pleasant and soothing scene, such as a green valley that you are looking down into from a mountaintop, watching a lazy brook meander its way through the valley, relaxing you more and more as you watch its slow movements. Another way is to imagine yourself descending a flight of stairs very slowly while thinking to yourself as you wind down the ancient stone stairwell that you are going deeper and deeper and deeper with each step. The following is an example of deepening the hypnotic trance state:

"I want you to imagine that you are standing on the fifth floor of a large department store ... and that you are just stepping into the elevator to descend to street level. And as you go down and as the elevator door opens and closes as you arrive at each floor ... you will become more and more deeply relaxed ... and your sleep will become deeper and deeper.

"The doors are closing now ... and you are beginning to sink slowly downwards.

"The elevator stops at the fourth floor ... several people get out ... two more get in ... the doors close again ... and already you are becoming more and more deeply relaxed ... more and more deeply asleep.

"And as you sink to the third floor ... and stop, while the doors open and close again ... you are relaxing more and more ... and your sleep is becoming deeper and deeper.

"You slowly sink down to the second floor ... one or two people get out and several get in ... and as they do so ... you are feeling much more deeply relaxed … much more deeply asleep.

"Down once again to the first floor … the doors open and close … but nobody gets out or in. Already you have become still more deeply relaxed … and your sleep still deeper and deeper. Deeper and deeper asleep … deeper and deeper asleep.

"Down further and further … until the elevator stops at last at street-level. The doors open … and everybody gets out.

"But you do not get out.

"You decide to go still deeper … and descend to the basement.

"The elevator doors close again … and down you go … down and down … deeper and deeper … and as you arrive at the basement … you are feeling twice as deeply and comfortably relaxed … twice as deeply asleep."

As you develop skill with your own mind, you will be able to go in trance much more quickly, and even surroundings that used to be too distracting for you to handle will now become tolerable for practicing self-hypnosis.

With each exposure to self-hypnosis, you will easily learn how to develop these relaxed states. The more exposure you receive, the easier and better it will be for you.

CHAPTER 15

SELF-HYPNOSIS SCRIPTS

❖

YOUR OWN MOTIVATION is the key to the success of this approach. The techniques are actually quite simple and anyone can apply them. You must truly want to accomplish these goals or else nothing will avail.

Over the years, I have found that the use of cassette tapes results in the most successful experiences with hypnosis. The transcripts given in this chapter can be used as a model for you to make your own tapes, as I explained in Chapter 5.

STANDARD HYPNOTIC INDUCTION

Ocean sounds alone for 10 seconds, then metronome beats in the background in sync with the voice.

"Sit back and listen to the beats of the metronome in the background. Each beat of the metronome will help you become more and more deeply relaxed. Listen as I count backwards from 20 to one. Each count backwards will get each and every muscle in your body so completely relaxed that when I reach the count of one, you will be at a very deep and relaxed level of hypnosis.

"20, 19, 18, deeply, deeply relaxed; 17, 16, 15, down, down, down; 14, 13, 12, very, very deep; 11, 10, 9, deeply, deeply relaxed; eight, seven, six, so very sleepy; five, four, three, deeply, deeply relaxed; 2, 1, deeply, deeply asleep. 20-20-20; you are now in a deeply relaxed level of hypnosis.

"Listen as I count backwards again, this time from seven to one. As I count backwards from seven to one you are going to hear the beats of the metronome in the background decrease in volume, decrease in volume with each count until I reach the count of one, at which time you will hear nothing but my voice. You will be in a very, very deep and relaxed level of hypnosis."

(Decrease metronome beats until the count of one, when they are gone completely.)

"Seven, deeper, deeper, deeper; down, down, down. Six, deeper, deeper, deeper; down, down, down. Five, deeper, deeper, deeper; down, down, down. Four, deeper, deeper, deeper; down, down, down. Three, deeper, deeper, deeper, down, down, down. Two, deeper, deeper, deeper, down, down, down. One, deeply, deeply, relaxed; deeply, deeply asleep. 20-20-20.

"You are now at a deeply relaxed level of hypnosis. The repetition of the number 20 three times in succession, 20-20-20, will quickly and very deeply get you into this nice deep level of hypnosis. This will get you quicker and deeper each and every time you practice self-hypnosis."

AGE REGRESSION

"Now listen very carefully. In a few minutes I'm going to be counting backwards from 20 to one, one more time. As I count backwards from 20 to one, you are going to perceive yourself moving through a very deep and dark tunnel. The tunnel will get lighter and lighter and at the very end of this tunnel will be a door with a bright white light above it.

"When you walk through this door you will be at an earlier age. You're going to re-experience this earlier age and move to an event that will be significant in explaining your present personality, or the origin of any problem or negative tendency.

"But before I do that, I want you to realize that if you feel uncomfortable either physically, mentally, or emotionally at any time you can awaken yourself from this hypnotic trance by simply counting forward from one to five. You will always associate my voice with a friendly voice in trance. You will be able to let your mind review back into its memory banks and to follow the instructions for perceiving the scenes from this earlier age, following along as I instruct.

"You'll find yourself able to get into hypnotic trances more deeply and more quickly each time you practice with this tape or with other methods of self-hypnosis. When you hear me say the words "Sleep now and rest," I want you to immediately detach yourself from any scene you are experiencing. You will be able to wait for further instructions.

"You absolutely have the power and ability to go back in time, as your subconscious mind's memory banks remembers everything you've ever experienced. I want you to relive these past events only as a neutral observer without feeling or emotion, just as if you were watching a television show. I want you to choose positive, neutral, or happy past experiences. You will be able to remove any obstacles that are preventing you from achieving your most useful, positive, beneficial and constructive goals.

"Go back and be able to explore at least two or three memories of yourself. It doesn't matter how far you go back. It doesn't matter what the years are. I just want you to get used to going backward in time.

"I'm going to count backwards now from 20 to one. As I do so, I want you to feel yourself moving into the past. You'll find yourself moving through a pitch-black tunnel that will get lighter and lighter as I count backwards. When I reach the count of one, you will have opened up a door with a bright white light above it and walked into a past scene. You will once again become yourself at an earlier age.

"Now listen carefully. 20, you're moving into a very deep, dark tunnel surrounded by grass and trees and flowers and a very, very inviting atmosphere. You feel very calm and comfortable about moving into the tunnel.

"19, 18, you're moving backwards in time, back, back.

"17, 16, 15, the tunnel is becoming lighter now. You can make out your arms and legs and you realize you are walking through this tunnel and you're moving backwards in time.

"14, 13, 12 moving so far back, back.

"11, 10, 9, you're so far back now, you're over halfway there. The tunnel is much lighter. You can perceive around you and you can now make out a door in front of you with a bright white light above it.

"Eight, seven six, standing in front of the door now, feeling comfortable and positive and confident about your ability to move into this past scene.

"Five, four, now walk up to the door and put your hand on the doorknob. The bright white light is so bright it's hard to look at.

"Three, open the door.

"Two, step through the door.

"One, move into the past scene. You are there.

"Focus carefully on what you see before you. Take a few minutes now and let everything become crystal clear. The information is flowing into your awareness, the scene is becoming visual and visible. Just take the time to orient yourself to your environment. Focus on it. Take a few moments and then listen to my instructions. Let the impressions form."

(Play music for 30 seconds.)

"First, what do you perceive and what are you doing? Focus carefully on my voice now. I want you to let any information—the scene as well as the actual environment you are in—flowing into your awareness become clear now. Crystal clear. I want you to focus on yourself. First of all, where you are. Focus on how old you are, how you are dressed, what you are doing there, your purpose there at this particular time, anyone else who is around you—parents, relatives, or friends. I'm going to give you a few moments. I want you to let the scene develop and become clear. Develop and become crystal clear."

(Play music for four minutes.)

"Sleep now and rest. Detach yourself from this scene now. I want you now to focus on my voice again. I'm going to be counting forwards again, this time from one to five. When I reach the count of five I want you to progress in time by three years. I want you to move at least three years farther forward in time.

"Move to a specific event that is going to happen to you. Something that is going to affect you and your development. I want you to move forward to a very significant scene. Especially if it involves other people.

"On the count of five now, I want you to perceive yourself in this scene just as you did before.

"One, moving forward, carefully, comfortably, slowly.

"Two, moving farther forward.

"Three, halfway there.

"Four, almost there.

"Five, you are there.

"Now focus again. Let the scene crystallize and become clear. Focus on yourself. Where you are? Who you are with? What is happening around you? What has happened since I last spoke with you? Understand the physical setting of the scene. Let it develop. Allow it to relate to your particular problem or just experience going back in time. Carefully, comfortably allow the scene to unfold. Carefully and comfortably. Now perceive the scene unfolding. Let it unfold now."

(Play music for four minutes.)

"Sleep now and rest. Now listen to my voice. Detach yourself from this scene. You're going to be moving forward one more time.

"On the count of five, you're going to be moving forward to a minimum of five years from this time. You will be moving forward to what ideally will be the resolution of this problem or to another significant scene that will affect the development of this problem or just to an experience of going back in time again.

"Moving forward to a minimum of five years from this time on the count of five. Carefully, comfortably.

"One, moving forward.

"Two, moving farther forward.

"Three, halfway there.

"Four, almost there.

"Five.

"Now, again, let the scene crystallize, become crystal clear. Focus on what is happening around you. Where are you; who are you with; what has happened since I last spoke with you? If this is a problem you are resolving, find out exactly what happened, exactly how it was resolved. Find out what additional facts are related to the present problem. Carefully and comfortably let the images flow and the scene become clear."

(Play music for four minutes.)

"All right, very good. You've done very well now. Sleep and rest.

Listen carefully as I count forward again from one to five. On the count of five, you will be back in the present. You will still be in a deep, hypnotic trance, but you will be able to relax comfortably and be free of these scenes. But you will still be in a trance.

"One, you're heading forward in time back to the present.

"Two, farther forward.

"Three, halfway there.

"Four, almost there.

"Five.

"Listen as I count forward one more time, from one to five. On the count of five, you will be wide awake, refreshed, relaxed. You will be able to do what you have planned for the rest of the day or evening. You will be able to remember everything you experienced and re-experienced, and be perfectly relaxed and at ease. You will also be able to re-create further experiences of scenes from the past by playing this tape again and again.

"One, very, very deep.

"Two, you're getting a little lighter.

"Three, you're getting much, much lighter.

"Four, very, very light.

"Five, awaken."

SELF-CONFIDENCE

"Every day ... you will become physically stronger and fitter. You will become more alert,...more wide awake,...more energetic. You will become much less easily tired,...much less easily fatigued,...much less easily discouraged.

"Every day ... your nerves will become stronger and steadier.

"You will become so deeply interested in whatever you are doing,...so deeply interested in whatever is going on,...that your mind will become much less preoccupied with yourself ... and you will become much less conscious of yourself ... and your own feelings.

"Every day ... your mind will become much calmer and clearer,... more composed,...more placid,...more tranquil. You will become much less easily worried,...much less easily agitated,...much less fearful and apprehensive,...much less easily upset.

"You will be able to think more clearly....You will be able to concentrate more easily....Your memory will improve,...and you will be able to see things in their true perspective,...without magnifying them,...without allowing them to get out of proportion.

"Every day ... you will become emotionally much calmer,...much more settled,...much less easily disturbed. And every day ... you will feel a greater feeling of personal well-being,...a greater feeling of personal safety and security ... than you have felt for a long, long time. Every day ... you will become ... and you will remain ... more and more completely relaxed ... both mentally and physically.

"And as you become ... and as you remain ... more relaxed ... and less tense each day,...you will develop much more confidence in yourself,...much more confidence in your ability to do ... not only what you have to do each day ... but also ... much more confidence in your ability to do whatever you ought to be able to do ... without fear of failure,...without fear of consequences,...without anxiety,...without uneasiness. Because of this,...every day ... you will feel more and more independent,...more able to "stick up for yourself," ... to stand upon your own two feet,...to hold your own, no matter how difficult or trying things may be.

"Every day, in every way, you are getting better, better, and better....Negative thoughts and negative suggestions have no influence over you at any mind level. And because all these things will happen ... exactly as I tell you they will happen,...you are going to feel much happier,...much more contented,...much more cheerful,...much more optimistic,...much less easily discouraged,...much less easily bothered."

STAGE FRIGHT

"As you become more relaxed and less tense each day,...so ... you will remain more relaxed and less tense ... when you are in the presence of other people,...no matter whether they be few or many,...no matter whether they be friends or strangers.

"You will be able to meet them on equal terms ... and you will feel much more at ease in their presence,...without the slightest feeling of inferiority ... without becoming self-conscious ... without becoming embarrassed or confused,...without feeling that you are making yourself conspicuous in any way.

"You will become so deeply interested,...so deeply absorbed in what you are doing and saying ... that you will concentrate on this entirely, to the complete exclusion of everything else.

"Because of this ... you will remain perfectly relaxed,...perfectly calm and self-confident,...and you will become much less conscious of yourself and your own feelings.

"You will thus be able to act and talk quite freely and naturally without being worried in the slightest by the presence of the others.

"If you should begin to think about yourself or have any negative thoughts, you will immediately shift your attention back to your conversation and you will no longer experience the slightest nervousness, discomfort, or uneasiness.

"The moment you get up to speak ... all your nervousness will disappear completely ... and you will feel completely relaxed,...completely at ease, and completely confident.

"You will become so deeply interested in what you have to say ... that the presence of an audience will no longer bother you in the slightest ... and you will no longer feel uncertain,...confused,...or conspicuous in any way.

"Your mind will become so fully occupied with what you have to say that you will no longer feel nervous,...self-conscious,...or embarrassed....And you will remain throughout ... perfectly calm,...perfectly confident, and self-assured.

"Whenever you are called upon to give a speech or talk, remember you must thoroughly prepare for it. You must master the topic and the delivery if you are to recite something. Rehearse thoroughly before the actual presentation.

"You will anticipate the performance with pleasurable expectation. During the performance, you will remain perfectly calm, poised, and self-confident. Your maximum ability and talents will surface.

"Any nervousness or anxiety will be transferred to the pinky finger of the left hand, which will become stiff and rigid. As the temporary nervousness disappears, the left pinky will relax and return to its normal condition."

STUDY HABITS AND MEMORY

"I am going to teach you how to concentrate. You have not been able to concentrate because nobody has even shown you exactly how to. I am going to show you exactly how to concentrate.

"Imagine yourself at your desk with the study material in front of you. Imagine closing your eyes and placing your hands over your ears. Now all noise and visual distractions are removed. As you think of the material to be studied, you will become more and more alert. Your breathing will become deep, regular and very, very slow.

"When you feel all distractions are gone, you will take two deep breaths. Your hands will drop to your sides, your eyes will open, and you will begin to concentrate entirely on the material in front of you,...nothing else. You may move your arms and legs or shift your position in the chair, and your concentration will remain undisturbed. If you are interrupted you may use this technique and be prepared to study once more. You will improve your concentration, be able to study longer, and absorb more this way.

"Think of your brain as a sponge. As a sponge soaks up water, so will your brain soak up knowledge; making an indelible mark in your mind so you will be able to recall it any time in the future. You will get twice as much work done in half the time.

"As you drift along, more and more deeply relaxed, concentrating your mind more and more, you are receptive to and you accept suggestions about memory and recall. The art of memory is the art of attention and retention. You must pay attention to anything in order to remember it. To remember something you must pay attention. When you concentrate your mind, you think, look, listen, associate, and remember.

"You must put information in your memory bank before you can recall it. You have an excellent memory and you are going to use it. You are going to pay close attention to everything you study from this moment on.

"Your memory bank is just like any other bank. It is not necessary to force your memory bank to give you information. You simply concentrate your mind, request the information, relax, and let it drift up to your conscious awareness.

"In order to recall anything, simply let your subconscious mind know exactly what you want. Anything you want to know then comes into your conscious awareness naturally and easily. If it does not come immediately, forget about it, and forget about the process of remembering. Do not try to force it. The information you want will come to your conscious awareness in a few moments....Sometimes when you least expect it, it will appear to pop into your mind. Any information you want comes into your conscious awareness ... naturally and easily.

"At the same time every evening you will study for a certain period of time. You will do nothing else for the allotted time. Nothing will interrupt you. If friends or family enter the room you will, with as much tact as possible, send them away. As you begin studying, your mind will quickly grasp the information at hand. Each important fact will make a profound impression on you. You will be able to recall information easily when future events demand it.

"Every day you will get into the habit of working for at least two hours without fail.

"You will be able to think more clearly....You will be able to concentrate much more easily.

"You will become so deeply interested and absorbed in what you are studying that you will be able to give your complete attention to what you are doing ... to the complete exclusion of everything else.

"Because of this ... you will be able to grasp things and understand them more quickly,...more easily, and they will impress themselves so deeply on your memory that you will not forget them.

"With every exposure to hypnosis and self-hypnosis that you have,...your memory will improve enormously and your work will become easier and easier. Your concentration will become greater and greater.

"You will not only be able to remember what you have learned,...but you will be able to recall it without difficulty ... whenever you need to do so.

"Your retention and attention span is increasing every day. Whatever you learn is permanently retained."

TEST TAKING

"The moment you enter the examination room and pick up your paper to read the questions ... you will become completely calm and relaxed ... and all your nervousness and apprehension will disappear completely. No matter how difficult some of the questions may seem at first sight … or how little you seem to know … you will not be disturbed,…because you will find that things are not as bad as they seem.

"Read all the questions carefully and deliberately.…Decide which one you can best answer, and answer that one as completely as you can … without worrying about the others until you have completed it. As you do this … you will find you actually remember far more than you originally thought you would.

"When you have put down all you know about this first question (or selected the correct choice) … choose the next easiest to answer … and handle that in exactly the same way. Continue in this way with the rest of the questions until you have written all you can remember (or selected all the correct choices) or until the time is up.

"You will find that by saying '20-20-20' you will quickly and deeply place yourself into a deep hypnotic trance and then you may ask your subconscious directly for information on answering any question. Then continue with the questions you can answer easily and you will find the answers to the more difficult questions simply pop into your mind."

INSOMNIA

"As you become more able to cope with and face up to the situations that have been causing your anxiety, then you will begin to sleep more easily and more soundly. There are no serious consequences to insomnia and the worries about the consequences of not sleeping are one of the main causes of this problem. If you do fall asleep so much the better! If you don't,…it doesn't matter, because sooner or later you will.

"Associate this relaxed feeling with bedtime relaxation. As a result of this treatment you will feel more relaxed, less tense and less anxious each day. As bedtime approaches, you will feel more and more pleasantly tired. You will go to bed at the same time each night and as soon as you put your head on the pillow you will begin to relax. You will no longer worry whether you are going to sleep or not. You will devote all your attention to totally relaxing. You are steadily losing your desire to wake up in the middle of the night; … you are steadily increasing your desire to fall asleep quickly and sleep through the night undisturbed.

"After you are in bed and just before you drop off to natural sleep, you will place yourself into a self-hypnotic trance by taking a deep breath, holding it to the count of 6, letting it out slowly and repeating the number 20 three times in succession and then telling yourself there is no need to take the day's problems to bed with you. As far as you are concerned, bed is for restful and healthful sleep, without dreams or thoughts that will disturb either your rest or your health. If you find yourself reliving a problem or negative situation, whether real or imaginary, you will put it out of your mind immediately and relax totally. You will reward yourself with this feeling of relaxation, which feels so very good.

"Now imagine a scene that you find most pleasant,...a scene you would rather be in if you had a choice....As soon as your head touches the pillow at night you will recreate this positive scene and enter into hypnosis and then quickly into natural sleep.

"If you should awaken in the middle of the night you will not be disturbed; ... simply take a deep breath, hold it to the count of six, let it out slowly, and repeat the number 20 three times and you will enter into hypnosis again and then quickly drift into natural sleep.

"You will fall asleep promptly and sleep soundly and restfully throughout the night. You will awaken in the morning refreshed, wide awake, well rested, and ready to start the day."

SMOKING

"You will have more self-control in the future. You will be able to smoke if you wish to smoke and you will be able to refrain from smoking, if you wish not to smoke. You will realize that smoking is a form of irritation and that the longer you go without a cigarette the less need you will have to smoke. One hour from now you will have less interest in smoking than you feel at this time. Two hours from now you will have less interest in smoking than you will have one hour from now. Thus, as each hour goes by you will have less interest, less desire, and less need to smoke.

"You have the utmost respect for your body. Smoking is poison. You need your body to live. You owe your body this respect and protection.

"You will be aware of smoking each time you light up a cigarette. You will no longer smoke by habit. You will weigh the advantages and disadvantages of smoking each time you are thinking about a cigarette.

"You will ignore the desire to smoke. Do not think at all about not smoking or smoking. If you repeatedly deny satisfaction to any urge, by ignoring it, the urge eventually goes away.

"From now on you will not smoke for one-half hour after awakening in the morning, before breakfast, within one-half hour after meals, and one-half hour before bed. [Lengthen this time as progress is made.] You will brush your teeth and use mouthwash at these times. The clean, fresh taste in your mouth is desirable, and you will want to do everything possible to maintain this state.

"Each cigarette you smoke will give you less and less pleasure. Associate this relaxation that you have now with a control over your own body through the use of your subconscious mind. You are steadily losing your desire for cigarettes.

"By giving up smoking, you will improve your health. You will be less likely to suffer from heart disease, emphysema, bronchitis, and lung cancer. Your digestion will improve and your food will taste better. However, you will not overeat because your self-confidence will improve also.

"Hold your breath for a slow count of ten. Let your breath out slowly and note how relaxed you are and note that you are breathing ordinary smokeless air. You will continue to be more relaxed as you breathe out ordinary smokeless air. You are in complete control of all of your habits. If the desire to smoke should arise, say to yourself, "I no longer smoke and I don't need to." The annoyances and irritation of everyday life are rolling off you like water off a duck's back.

"Nicotine is a poison.

"Smoking is harmful to everyone's health–this is an established fact.

"Anyone can stop smoking....You have the power to stop smoking permanently.

"Excessive smoking increases nervous tension; ... it doesn't decrease it.

"Whenever you are tempted to smoke, you will automatically ask yourself if you really want to indulge yourself. If you do you will, but you will find you prefer to exercise the hypnotic techniques and suggestions that I have given you to eliminate the cause, desire, and need for smoking cigarettes."

WEIGHT REDUCTION

"Being overweight is unhealthy.

"You need your body to live.

"You owe your body this respect and protection.

"You have the power to reprogram your subconscious mind to reverse the prior thoughts of overeating and thinking of yourself as overweight. You will, starting today, reprogram your subconscious to think of yourself as thin and will eat only the foods that are healthy and necessary for your body.

"You are going to lose all the weight you desire to lose, and you are going to do it starting today. I want you to associate this relaxed state that you are now in with a relaxed attitude about losing weight. Don't count calories. As you lose weight you will gain more confidence and find further weight reduction easier. When you eat you will cut your food into small pieces and chew them slowly and completely before swallowing. Eat only one mouthful of food at a time. You will find that by eating slowly and smaller portions, you will enjoy your meals better and eat less food. You will find that half way through a meal you will feel full. When this happens you will stop eating. You will never, ever, eat when you are not hungry.

"Repeat these statements to yourself:

1.   I will get more filling satisfaction from less food every day.

2.   I will eat slowly and only at mealtimes,...sparingly and properly.

3.   I am losing weight steadily every week.

4.   I am becoming slim and shapely.

5.   I have a stronger feeling every day that I am in complete control of my eating habits.

6.   I am developing a greater liking every day for the foods that make me slim and shapely.

"Remember, if you repeatedly deny satisfaction to a hunger pang, the desire eventually goes away.

"From this moment on you will not think of yourself as being overweight. Every time such a thought comes into your mind, it programs your subconscious negatively. So you will now monitor your thoughts. Any thoughts or actions that come into your mind about being overweight will be canceled out by saying to yourself, "I am thin. I am thin." From this moment on you are going to eat only those foods necessary to keep you healthy and mentally alert. You are going to eat smaller portions of the foods necessary to keep you mentally alert and healthy. You will desire no more.

"You will be totally aware of eating,...will no longer eat by habit. From this moment on you will no longer eat between meals, or while watching TV, and you will have absolutely no desire to eat between meals or while watching TV.

"You are going to set a realistic goal for your weight loss and you will carry it out successfully. Decide how many pounds (kilos) you can realistically lose every week and you will lose this exact amount. Now repeat to yourself the realistic amount you can lose each week until you reach your ideal weight.

"You will find it easier and easier every day to stick to a reducing diet. You will enjoy smaller meals. The irritation and annoyances of everyday life are rolling off you, like water off a duck's back. You will thoroughly enjoy the foods that are good for you and healthy also.

"Remember, four important things are going to happen. First of all,...relaxation. Every day ... you will become ... and will remain more relaxed and less tense. That relaxation will lead to greater calmness. Every day you will become calmer ... and more composed. That increased feeling of calmness will result in greatly increased confidence. Every day ... you will feel more confident,...more self-assured. And that confidence will lead to much greater power of self-control. You will gain much more control over the way you think,...over the way you feel,...over the way you behave.

"You will begin to enjoy more and more the sight,...the smell,...as well as the taste and flavor only of the foods that are good for you....You will gradually lose your craving for those that will lead to the accumulation of fat, retention of fluids.

"Even when you cut out carbohydrates (including cakes and pastries),...foods rich in starch,...sweets, etc.,...there are still plenty of appetizing foods ... salads and fruits, among others,...that will begin to appeal to you more and more ... as you eat more slowly,...thus really enjoying the sight,...smell,...and flavor of what you eat. Consequently, you will no longer be tempted into eating between meals ... and will have less and less difficulty in avoiding foods that are fattening.

"You will exercise more each day and drink more water ... and as you gradually lose weight ... you will become much healthier and fitter ... and your personal appearance will improve.

"Every day ... your desire and determination to stick to your diet ... and change your former eating habits will increase,...to such an extent that it will completely overwhelm any temptation to depart from it....The temptation will eventually disappear.

"Some people fear being thin. But you don't have to fear losing weight. No matter why you gained the weight, for whatever reasons you became a compulsive eater, it is no longer important. What is important is that you have decided to change your eating habits, so that you can reach your desired goal—the image, shape, weight and size that you desire. It doesn't really matter whether you are fat or become thin. You are still the same person. You still have the same power, the same personality, the same inner reality, no matter what your body shape, weight, or size is. There is no need to fear losing any of yourself when you lose weight. As the weight and inches (cm) roll off, as you control your eating habits, you remain the same you, only more trim. You do not need to fear that you are losing any of your protection. You are the same person.

"Don't wait till you lose all the weight to become the person you want to be if you want to be someone different. Wear the clothes now that project your image. Sit, walk, act with your thin personality. Don't worry about hiding the fat. Wearing fat clothes doesn't hide the fat. That only makes you feel worse. So wear the clothes you want to wear, that project the real you now, as you are losing weight. This will reinforce your desire to reach your goal.

"As that extra weight begins to roll off, melt away, disappear, you are totally comfortable with your emerging slender and shapely body. You are perfectly contented and at ease with the emerging slim, trim, and slender you. You are in control of your eating habits. You are in control of your life, you are in control of losing weight, and you are in control of your personality and your body. You are perfectly happy with the inner you that remains as you lose weight and inches (cm).

"I truly believe that you are capable of dieting successfully and effortlessly to achieve and maintain your ideal weight of *(specify the amount)*. You will be guided by the natural powers within you to achieve and maintain this healthy and attractive body.

"Whenever you are tempted to eat fattening food or violate any of these suggestions, you will automatically ask yourself if you really want to indulge. If you do you will, but you will find that you will prefer to exercise the hypnotic techniques and suggestions that I have given you to reach and maintain your ideal weight."

PAIN AND HEALING

"As you relax more and more, in hypnosis and self-hypnosis, the relaxation causes all the muscles and nerves in the affected area to become completely relaxed, thus relieving the symptom and causing the pain to disappear. As you become more and more relaxed in every way, you return to normal functioning and your body feels completely comfortable and free from all discomfort.

"You are becoming desensitized in the various parts of your body where you have been complaining of pain. You will now find yourself recovering rapidly, the healing process greatly facilitated thanks to the recruitment of nature's healing forces.

"Naturally, the pain will not stop all at once, but you will find it lessening substantially each and every day. Any time you feel particularly uncomfortable, and this may happen for a few days, you will merely make yourself comfortable, close your eyes, and say '20-20-20.'

"The act of counting is a post-hypnotic suggestion intended to relieve the discomfort. The act of counting will cause you to become desensitized and anesthetized in those parts of the body where you are uncomfortable and you will rapidly resume a relaxed and comfortable condition.

"You will also find yourself pleasantly hungry at mealtimes and will be able to eat well and hold your food down satisfactorily. [This latter suggestion was given if there is nausea.] You are steadily losing your desire for pain and discomfort.

"Feel yourself becoming a loving and forgiving person. Consider love as an end in itself. Express your desire to achieve a thorough mental house cleaning....Use positive words and positive thoughts to become a loving, forgiving person.

"Imagine the illness or pain bothering you. Focus your healing energies. Quickly erase this image of your illness and see yourself completely cured. Feel the freedom and happiness of being in perfect health. Hold on to this image, linger over it, enjoy it, and know that you deserve it. Know that now in this healthy state you are fully in tune with nature's intentions for you.

"Every day, in every way you are getting better, better, and better. Negative thoughts and negative suggestions have no influence over you at any mind level."

See the glove anesthesia script for an additional pain elimination technique.

DENTAL FEAR

"Your muscles are tight rubber bands that are progressively unwinding and becoming looser and looser. This will continue until you feel that every bit of tension is gone or until they are as loose and relaxed as you want them to be today. This wonderful relaxation will be such a help to you, you will be very comfortable during your next dental appointment. At future appointments you will notice the muscles of your body beginning to unwind as soon as you enter the office.

"When you are seated in the dental chair you will think of the number 20 three times in succession and immediately feel the relaxation developing. The dental chair will feel very soft and comfortable and will remind you of your favorite resting chair at home.

"Concentrate on enjoying this wonderful relaxed feeling. The various sounds and noises that you will hear will have the same soothing effect as listening to your favorite music.

"Your fears of a dental appointment will cease to exist.

"You will be able to allow the necessary dental treatment to be carried out.

"You will experience no fear whatsoever during the entire time you spend with the dentist.

"You will experience no fear whatsoever during appointments in which teeth have to be removed, filled, etc.

"You are steadily losing your desire to be afraid of a dentist or dental procedures."

GAGGING

"During all dental procedures you will be relaxed, calm, comfortable, and you will experience only a normal gag reflex. The excessive gag reflex will be eliminated and you will remain relaxed, calm, and comfortable during dental procedures."

GRINDING TEETH (BRUXISM)

"Whenever you grind your teeth or tighten your cheek muscles, you will want to keep your mouth slightly open, wide enough to place your tongue between your back teeth. This will help your muscles to become loose, loose....This will stop your muscles from cramping. The longer your tongue stays between your teeth, the more your muscles will become loose, limp, like wet cotton.

"From now on as you continue your relaxation into sleep, let your mind dwell on the phrase, 'Lips together, teeth apart.' In addition, when you feel the need to grind or clench your teeth, clench your fists instead."

DENTAL OFFICE VISIT

"As I talk to you for a moment about something you already know a lot about,...remembering and forgetting,...you know a lot about it, because we all do a lot of it....Every moment of every day you remember ... and then you forget, so you can remember something else....You can't remember everything all at once, so you let some memories move quietly back in your mind....

"I wonder, for instance, if you remember what you had for lunch yesterday....I would guess that, with not too much effort, you can remember what you had for lunch yesterday ... and yet,...I wonder if you remember what you had for lunch a month ago today....I would guess the effort is really too great to dig up that memory, though of course it is there ... somewhere, deep in the back of your mind.

"No need to remember, so you don't; ... and I wonder if you'll be pleased to notice that the things we talk about today, with your eyes closed, are things you'll remember tomorrow, or the next day,...or next week....I wonder if you'll decide to let the memory of these rest quietly in the back of your mind ... or if you'll remember gradually, a bit at a time,...or perhaps all at once, to be again resting in the back of your mind....

"Perhaps you'll be surprised to notice that the reception room is the place for memory to surface,...perhaps not....Perhaps you'll notice that it is more comfortable to remember on another day altogether; ... it really doesn't matter,...doesn't matter at all....

"Whatever you do, however you choose to remember ... is just fine,...absolutely natural,...doesn't matter at all....Whether you remember tomorrow or the next day, whether you remember at once or gradually ... completely or only partially; ... whether you let the memory rest quietly and comfortably in the back of your mind ... really doesn't matter at all,...and, too, I wonder if you'll notice that you'll feel surprised that your visit here today is so much more pleasant and comfortable than you might have expected....

"I wonder if you'll notice that surprise ... that there are no other feelings....Perhaps you'll feel curious about that surprise,...surprise, curiosity,...I wonder if you'll be pleased to notice that today ... and any day,...whenever you feel your head resting back against a dental chair,...when you feel your head resting back like this,...you'll feel reminded of how very comfortable you are feeling right now ... even more comfortable than you feel even now,...comfortable, relaxed,...nothing to bother, nothing to disturb....

"I wonder if you'll be reminded of this comfort, too, and relaxation, by just noticing the brightness of the light on the ceiling....Perhaps this comfort and relaxation will come flooding back, quickly and automatically, whenever you find yourself beginning to sit down in the dental chair....

"I don't know exactly how it will seem,...I only know, as perhaps you also know,...that your experience will seem surprisingly more pleasant, surprisingly more comfortable, surprisingly more restful than you might expect,...with nothing to bother you, nothing to disturb you....

"Whatever you are able to notice,...everything can be a part of your experience of comfort, restfulness, and,, and relaxation....Everything you notice can be a part of being absolutely comfortable,...and I want to remind you that whenever you say '20-20-20,' ... whenever it is appropriate, and only when it is appropriate,...whenever you say '20-20-20' to yourself,...a feeling,...a feeling of being ready to do something,...perhaps a feeling of being ready to close your eyes,...perhaps a feeling of being ready to be even more comfortable,...perhaps ready to know even more clearly that there's nothing to bother, nothing to disturb,…perhaps ready to become heavy and tired,…I don't know,…but whenever you say '20-20-20,' … you'll experience a feeling,…a feeling of being ready to do something.…It really doesn't matter; … perhaps just a feeling of being ready to be even more surprised,…it doesn't really matter.…

"Nothing really matters but your experience of comfort and relaxation,…absolute deep comfort and relaxation … with nothing to bother and nothing to disturb.…That's fine … and now, as you continue to enjoy your comfortable relaxation, I'd like you to notice how very nice it feels to be this way,…to really enjoy your own experience, to really enjoy the feelings your body can give you.…"

You can now use this training to be relaxed during your next visit to the dentist.

GLOVE ANESTHESIA

"All feeling is going to disappear from your right hand. You will not be able to feel anything in your right hand.…Just think of your right hand becoming quite numb … as if it had gone to sleep. Gradually … it is becoming more and more numb … and all the feeling is going out of it.

"And as I go on talking to you … your right hand is beginning to feel colder and colder … as if it were surrounded by ice.

"Just picture your right hand being packed with ice.…And as you do so … it is feeling colder and colder,…more and more numb and insensitive.

"Your right hand has now become so cold and numb … that you are losing all feeling in it. Soon, you will not be able to feel any sensation in it at all.

"In a moment or two … I am going to count slowly to three. And when I reach the count of three,…your right hand will be completely insensitive to pain … and you will be able to feel no pain at all in your hand. One,…losing all sensation of pain. Two,…your hand is now quite numb and dead.…There is no feeling in it at all,…just as if it had gone to sleep. Three,…your hand is completely numb,…cold,…and insensitive.…You cannot feel any pain in it at all.

"Now use your right hand to touch any part of your body that is painful. By doing so, all this cold, numb feeling from your right hand and fingers will be transferred to this part of your body. Do it now.

"In a few moments ... your right hand will become quite normal again. It is becoming warmer and warmer ... and the feeling of numbness is leaving it ... and it is quite normal again,...just the same as your other hand.

"All sensation has returned ... and you can feel everything,... just the same as with your left hand. However, the cold, numb feeling will remain in the part of your body your right hand touched until the cause of the discomfort has been removed by your body's healing processes."

SKIN PROBLEMS

"As a result of this treatment ... you are going to feel stronger and fitter in every way.

"Your circulation will improve,...particularly the circulation through the little blood vessels that supply the skin.

"Your heart will beat more strongly ... so that more blood will flow through the little blood vessels in the skin,...carrying more nourishment to the skin. Because of this,...your skin will become much better nourished ... it will become healthier,...more normal in texture,...and the rash* will gradually diminish ... until it fades away completely,...leaving the underlying new skin perfectly healthy and normal in every respect.

"And ... as your circulation improves ... and your nerves become stronger and steadier,...so ... they will become much less sensitive ... and much less easily irritated.

"Consequently ... the itching and irritation of your skin will gradually subside ... and disappear.

"It will become less and less each day ... and you will no longer have any desire to scratch.

"If ... at any time,...unknowingly, you do begin to scratch ... the moment your fingers touch your skin ... you will immediately know what you are about to do ... and you will be able to exercise sufficient self-control to stop yourself ... before you have done any damage at all.

*For acne, substitute the word "pimples" or "acne" for "rash," and delete the reference to itching and scratching.

"Because of this ... you will not only feel much less irritation and discomfort,...but your skin will begin to heal ... and your rash will begin to disappear much more rapidly.

"Even if you should start to scratch ... in your sleep at night ... the moment your fingers touch your skin ... you will wake up immediately and realize exactly what you are doing ... and will be able to stop yourself.

"And ... because of this treatment ... you will be able to exercise enough control to stop scratching at all times ... before you have done any damage to your skin. You are steadily losing your desire for skin problems."

HEADACHES

"Today is a very important day to you ... because it is the first day of the rest of your life. I am speaking of the rest of your life without your usual headache, because from today forward you will begin to notice a change in the usual pattern of your headache and you will never have that same headache again.

"Your headaches will become less frequent, and less severe in intensity and duration ... less frequent and less severe ... until they disappear ... and they will disappear, when you decide they will.

"As you become more confident in yourself, you will no longer fear your headache, because you no longer will allow it to control your way of life. Consequently you will come to disrespect it, and it will feel unwelcome and disappear.

"I am sure you have often asked yourself what the cause of your headache is. I tell you it is a bad habit you have learned over the years. You weren't born with it. The reason you are having headaches now may not be the reason you started having them several years ago.

"Good or bad habits are learned, and what your mind can learn it can unlearn. You are going to unlearn this bad habit of having headaches, and replace it with the good habit of not having headaches. But, like changing any habit, it takes determination, and the fact that you are here tells me that you have this required determination.

"A headache is not a disease. But like all pain it is a warning or a symptom that something is not right in the body. A headache is a symptom that you are having trouble coming to terms with your environment, losing your ability to cope with the everyday, changing surroundings.

"In other words, if you are able to control your emotions instead of letting your emotions control you, you would never have another headache.

"In the future, each time you start to ruminate about some problem, either real or imaginary, you will immediately become aware of it. This is the first step, and it's half the battle won. You will put it out of your mind and relax on the spot, and reward yourself with this feeling of relaxation, which feels so good, as you are now becoming aware. This mechanism will become automatic very quickly if you work at it.

"There are times in the day when you are predisposed to rumination. Learn to recognize them and relax when you spot them. Some of these times are: when someone has kept you waiting, disappointed you, criticized you, or rejected you. You should also learn to relax in traffic jams and at red lights.

"Incidentally, you will find that you are changing, and that you are no longer feeding on your grudges. You are beginning to mature and grow. This will give you self-confidence, and your headaches will be gone.

"After you are in bed, just before you drop off to sleep, put yourself in a state of self-hypnosis and tell yourself there is no need to take the day's problems to bed with you. As far as you are concerned, bed is restful and healthful sleep without dreams that will disturb either your rest or your health. You will not awaken with a headache; you will awaken instead refreshed and relaxed both mentally and physically.

"Whenever you feel that an attack is beginning … stop whatever you are doing,…lie back in a chair,…and put yourself in deep hypnosis by saying '20-20-20.'"

NAIL BITING

"You are a very attractive person. You do not want your appearance to be spoiled by ugly hands. Nice hands and shapely nails will make you even more attractive … and you will want to make every effort to stop biting your nails and spoiling them.

"You will be able to stop biting them altogether … and then they will soon begin to grow. As your nerves become stronger and steadier,…as you become calmer and more relaxed each day,…there will be no reason for you to go on biting your nails.

"By using self-hypnosis … you will no longer want to bite them.…You will stop biting them. If, at any time, you do start to bite them without realizing what you are doing … the moment your fingers touch your mouth … you will know immediately what you are doing … and you will be able to stop yourself right away … before you have done any damage.

"From now on … you will stop biting your nails.…They will begin to grow, and you will begin to feel proud of your hands.

"You owe your body this respect and protection. You will weigh the pros and cons each time you are about to bite your nails. Associate relaxation over your muscles now with control over your habits. Do not think about nail biting. If you repeatedly deny satisfaction to an urge or desire by ignoring it, it eventually goes away.

"Whenever your hand starts to move toward your mouth for the purpose of biting your nails, you will become aware of it before it reaches your mouth. You then say to yourself … or aloud,…'Do I really want to bite my nails?' If your answer is 'yes,' then go ahead and enjoy it! But chances are, when you are aware of doing something so foolish, you'd rather not,…so you won't.

"You are in complete control of all your habits. If the desire to bite your nails arises, you will say to yourself, 'I no longer bite my nails, and I don't need to,' then think of the pleasant scene. You are steadily losing your desire to bite your nails."

PHOBIAS

"As you continue to relax, automatically going deeper and deeper, I want you to picture yourself relaxing at home in your favorite chair, just watching TV or just listening to your favorite music. Now I want you to picture yourself, as best you can, in the most relaxing environment you have ever experienced,... Keep this image as a reference point and go back to it when I say 'relax.'

"Now I want you to perceive yourself being exposed to what you fear, but to a very small degree. This scene represents the weakest association with your phobia. Do this now....Now relax and think of the pleasant scene you created earlier.

"Now I want you to see yourself being placed in the phobic situation to a greater degree. Do this now with complete confidence....Relax now and see how much control your mind has over your body."

(Continue with four to six more advanced phobic scenes.)

"Relax once more. Now you will be able to apply this technique in real life. The next time you are exposed to the phobic environment, your anxiety level will be much lower and you will be able to relax by using this simple exercise. Each time you are exposed to what you fear, your fearful response will decrease until soon it will disappear completely."

ANXIETY

"Relaxation will give you the peace of mind and inner tranquillity that will enable you to cope with the tensions and stresses of everyday living.

"You will be able to adjust yourself to your environment even though you may not be able to change it.

"You will be able to tolerate the persons, places, or things that used to disturb and annoy you.

"You can do everything better when you are relaxed, whether it be physical, mental or emotional.

"You can and will control your entire body with your subconscious mind. Imagine controlling the muscles of your tongue, and you won't say things you will be sorry for in the future.

"Relaxation will give you all the courage and confidence you need to take the 'T' out of 'can't' and find out that you can and will. Want it to happen; expect it to happen; and it will happen.

"You are steadily losing your desire to be anxious. You are steadily increasing your desire to remove all emotional discomforts and become a completely empowered person.

"As each of your worries is eliminated, it will not be replaced by another."

DREAM CONTROL

While in hypnosis, just before going to sleep, say to yourself, "I want to remember a dream. I will remember a dream." Keep a cassette player ready to record or a pen and pad by your bed. When you awaken, dictate or write down what you remember of the dream. Keep practicing this night after night and you will recall these dreams in more and more detail.

While in hypnosis, just before going to sleep, review a problem that can be solved with information or advice. Be sure you really care about solving it. Now say to yourself, "I want to have a dream that will contain information to solve a problem, such as *(specify)*. I will have such a dream, remember it, and understand it."

ALLERGY

"As you become more relaxed and less tense each day ... you will remain more relaxed and less tense ... when you are in the presence of _____. You will be able to handle _____ with much more ease without the slightest side effect or allergic response.

"Because of this, you will remain perfectly relaxed,...perfectly calm and self-confident,...and you will automatically shift your attention back to this relaxed state that you are in now and you will not experience these allergic responses of _____.

"Every day your nerves will become stronger and stronger. You will become so deeply interested in whatever you are doing that your mind will become much less preoccupied with allergic responses to _____ and you will become less conscious of the presence of _____.

"Every day ... you will become emotionally calmer,...much more settled,...much less easily disturbed. Every day ... you will feel a greater feeling of personal well-being,...a greater feeling of personal safety and security and a freedom from allergic responses to _____.

"As you become and as you remain ... more relaxed ... and less tense each day ... so will you develop more confidence in yourself,...much more confidence in your ability to free yourself from these allergic responses to _____ without fear of failure.

"Because all of these things will happen ... exactly as I tell you they will happen ... you are going to feel much happier,...much more contented,...much more cheerful,...much more optimistic,...much less easily discouraged,...much less easily depressed.

"From this moment on you are no longer allergic to _____. You are no longer allergic to _____. You no longer respond to _____ with _____.

"You are steadily losing your desire for allergic responses to _____.

ASTHMA

"Now that you are relaxed in self-hypnosis, I want you to count backwards from 20 to one.

"On each count, I want you to inhale deeply, clenching your fists as you do so. Relax your fists when you exhale. Do this three times a day.

"You are steadily losing your desire for asthma symptoms.

"Whenever you feel an attack coming on ... just as soon as you get the first indications ... you will take a deep breath and go into hypnosis by saying '20-20-20.'

"You will then immediately start your exercise ... inhale, clench your fists, exhale, and relax. This should prevent the attack ... or if the attack does develop, it should be much milder than usual.

"While you are doing this, you are to keep counting backward from 20 to one. When you have reached the count of one, you will count up from one to five and awaken feeling refreshed, wide awake, and free of all discomfort."

STUTTERING

"You are only going to concern yourself with the last syllable or letters of a word. This way, you will find it very easy to pronounce the first few letters or syllables.

"If possible, look directly into the face of the person you are speaking to. If it is a telephone conversation, then mentally picture looking directly at him or her.

"Imagine yourself listening to yourself speaking on a wide variety of subjects without hesitation and without stuttering. Practice speaking out loud slowly but deliberately for 15 minutes per day when you are alone.

"You are gradually losing your desire to stutter.

"You know you can speak properly when you are speaking out loud to yourself if you are alone in a room. Actually, you can speak perfectly, if you speak very slowly and carefully.

"You only stutter when you are nervous or excited and try to speak too rapidly. In the future you will have more self-control, and you will speak bit more slowly and carefully, and you will find that you will be speaking more properly.

"You do not stutter when you are singing. That is because when you are singing, you are speaking with a rhythm. For the next few days you can practice speaking with a rhythm.

"You can tap your finger on the table and say, 'One, two, three, four, I will speak more carefully and more slowly.' You say each word as you tap your finger and you will be speaking properly.

"After a few days of speaking in this manner you will soon forget that you once had speech defect and you will find yourself speaking as well any of your friends. You will see a gradual improvement in your ability to speak slowly and carefully and you will be well pleased.

FRIGIDITY

"I am getting more pleasure and enjoyment from making love.

"During intercourse, I am completely relaxed and uninhibited.

"It's easier and easier to enjoy intercourse, excited yet relaxed.

"It will be easier and easier to be more relaxed and confident at each sexual experience.

"You are steadily losing your desire to be frigid.

"Your partner is a good man but he cannot help his critical attitude, since it is due largely to his early training and upbringing.

"You will find yourself able to make allowances for him and you will learn to ignore what you consider his criticisms. In fact, you will find the irritations and the annoyances of the situation rolling off you like water off a duck's back.

"You are developing sufficient ego strength to become invulnerable to these annoyances. As a result, your sexual responses are returning to normal and you are functioning normally and naturally. Your vagina is becoming more lubricated as you think of making love and when you partner is with you.

"When you are making love, you are always relaxed and at ease. Your mind is imbued with feelings of pleasure, causing you to act normally and naturally.

"Sex should not be regarded as a performance, but an act both partners derive pleasure from, so feelings of pleasure–of loving and being loved–saturate your mind, causing your behavior to be normal and natural. Sex is normal and natural. Enjoying sex is normal and natural."

IMPOTENCE AND PREMATURE EJACULATION

"It will be easier and easier to be more relaxed and confident at each sexual experience.

"It is easier and easier to enjoy making love, excited yet relaxed.

"It is easy to last (maintain an erection) as long as you wish.

"You are getting more pleasure and enjoyment from making love every time.

"During intercourse, you are completely relaxed and uninhibited.

"You are steadily losing your desire to be impotent and/or to ejaculate prematurely.

"When you are making love, you are always relaxed and at ease. Your mind is filled with feelings of pleasure, causing you to act normally and naturally.

"Sex should not be regarded as a performance, but an act from which both partners derive pleasure, so feelings of pleasure–of loving and being loved–saturate your mind, causing your behavior to be normal and natural. Sex is normal and natural. Enjoying sex is normal and natural."

ARTHRITIS

"Your whole arm is gradually becoming more relaxed. Both your elbow and fingers will feel more comfortable. As you relax more and more, your arm and hands will feel better than they have for a long time.

"Your body processes will become more efficient and your blood and tissue fluids will carry away the impurities and waste products from your body. This will relieve the clogging in your joints.

"Any remaining discomfort can easily be moved to your upper arm so your elbow and hands will feel perfectly comfortable. You are able to do this at any time.

"Every time you move your arm a drop of lubrication will be secreted. This will help make you more comfortable. There will be a slow, gradual improvement, but you will notice the improvement each time you move your arm and you will be pleased to notice your recovery.

"You are steadily losing your desire for arthritis symptoms."

ALCOHOLISM

"From now on, you will want to give up drinking altogether. Your desire and determination to give it up will become so strong, so powerful, it will completely overwhelm your craving to drink. You will begin to feel a strong dislike for alcohol in any form.

"Every day … your craving will become less and less,…weaker and weaker,…until it disappears completely. You will realize … more and more … that alcohol is a poison to you.

"Whenever you feel that you simply must have a drink,…sucking on a hard candy, which you will carry with you at all times from now on, will immediately remove the urge to drink, and you will quickly become both relaxed and comfortable. Thinking of the number 20 three times will also increase this feeling of comfort and relaxation.

"You have the power to stop drinking. Just as you have the power to relax every muscle in your body, as you are doing now, so you can control any and all of your habits, including drinking.

"You will stop drinking as soon as you desire to. And it will be because you really want to do so, down deep inside. I am only a friend who wishes to guide you as long as you need me.

"With each passing day, your desire to drink is going to become less and less....

"With each passing day, you are going to feel stronger and stronger as a person, and your need to drink will be correspondingly decreased....

"With each passing day, you are going to derive more and more pleasure out of life, and so you will have less and less need to dull your senses with alcohol.

"If you should ever feel a need to take a drink of alcohol, just say '20-20-20' and this urge will lessen and disappear.

"The next time you are at a party where alcoholic drinks are served, you are going to find that a soft drink will satisfy your craving just as much as one that contains alcohol....Soft drinks by themselves will completely satisfy your desire to drink....

"You will be able to enjoy yourself and have a good time at the party without consuming any alcohol whatsoever....And any time your craving should return momentarily, another soft drink will completely eliminate it once more....

"You will remain completely sober throughout the entire evening,... and afterwards, you will realize that you had a much more enjoyable time than you would have had if you had been drinking.

"You are steadily losing your desire for alcohol.

BLUSHING

"As you become more relaxed ... and less tense each day,...so ... you will remain more relaxed ... and completely at ease ... when you are in the presence of other people,...no matter whether they be few or many,...no matter whether they be friends or strangers.

"You will be able to meet them on equal terms,...to talk to them quite easily ... without feeling self-conscious,...without feeling embarrassed,...without becoming confused,...without feeling conspicuous in any way.

"You will be more self-confident,...more self-assured,...and so deeply interested in what you have to say ... that you will be much less conscious of yourself ... and of your own feelings.

"And because you will remain emotionally calm and undisturbed,...you will no longer blush nearly as easily ... or as frequently.

"If you do feel yourself beginning to blush … you will not become worried, uneasy, or confused.…You will be able to ignore it completely … and carry on the conversation without letting it disturb you in the least.

"And because of this … it will die away, very, very rapidly indeed,…so that it will pass almost unnoticed by others.

"The less notice you take of it,…the less frequently and intensely it will occur.…And with each treatment … it will happen less and less … until, eventually, it will no longer happen at all.

"You are steadily losing your desire to blush."

BED-WETTING

"As a result of this deep sleep, you are going to feel stronger and better every day. You will become much calmer,…much quieter,…much less easily excited,…much less nervous,…much less easily upset.

"Every day, you will feel much more confidence in yourself.…You will feel more able to stick up for yourself … without becoming worried,…without becoming frightened,…without becoming upset.

"As you stroke your tummy … you will get a feeling of warmth in your tummy.…Your tummy is getting warmer and warmer, with every stroke of your hand.

"And as you continue to stroke your tummy, that warmth is spreading deep down into the lower part of your tummy,…into the bladder, which holds your water.

"And, as your bladder becomes warmer … so, it is becoming stronger,…so that it will be able to hold your water all night long, and in the morning your bed will be dry. With every treatment, you will become stronger and stronger …

"You will never have anything to drink just before your bedtime. You will always remember to go to the bathroom immediately before you get into bed. You won't worry about whether you will have a dry bed or not, because there will be no need for you to do so.…And the less you worry about it,…the quicker the bed will become dry.

"You will sleep well,…but you will not sleep so deeply.…If there is any need for you to go to the bathroom during the night, your tummy will begin to feel so uncomfortable you will wake up with plenty of time to get out of bed and relieve yourself in the proper place. When you get back into bed again, you will fall asleep right away....And when you wake up in the morning, your bed will be dry.

"During the daytime, whenever you feel you want to relieve yourself, I want you to hold it back, as long as you can,...and only go to the toilet when you feel you can't possibly last much longer.

"If you get into the habit of doing this, you will find that you will gradually be able to hold your water longer and longer during the day,...and as this happens, you will be able to hold it longer and longer during the night ... all night long, in fact ... so that in the morning your bed will be dry.

"Whenever you do go to the toilet during the day, as soon as you have started, I want you to get into the habit of stopping yourself before you have finished ... starting again ... then stopping again ... and then finishing completely. If you do this, it will help you to get complete control over it, even during the night. You are steadily losing your desire to wet your bed.

"And because these things will happen ... exactly as I tell you they will happen ... you will feel much happier,...much more contented,... much less easily worried,...much less easily upset."

GAINING WEIGHT

"Being underweight is unhealthy.

"You need your body to live.

"You owe your body this respect and protection.

"You have the power to reprogram your subconscious to reverse the prior thoughts of undereating and thinking of yourself as being underweight. You will, starting today, reprogram your subconscious to thinking of yourself as weighing your ideal weight of _____ and eating only those foods that are healthy for your body.

"You are going to gain all the weight you desire until you reach your ideal weight of _____ and you are going to do this starting today.

"I want you to see yourself as you desire to be. See yourself at your ideal weight of _____. You have the power to create your own reality. See yourself as weighing your ideal weight and you will reach this weight.

"See others around you admiring your new weight and complimenting you on how good you look. This is your reality, and starting today your subconscious mind will begin making this reality come true.

"I want you to associate this relaxed state you are in right now with a relaxed attitude about gaining weight.

"After you finish a meal you will still be hungry. You will eat larger portions of the foods that are healthy and necessary for your body.

"I want you to say to yourself, 'I am gaining weight steadily every day.' Right now I want you to set a realistic goal for gaining weight. Decide right now how much you can realistically gain each week and you will gain this exact amount. Now repeat to yourself the realistic amount of weight you can gain each week to reach your ideal weight of _____.

"You are steadily losing your desire to be underweight."

WARTS

"I want you to stroke your hand that displays warts. As you stroke your hand, you can feel a feeling of warmth spreading into the skin of your hand. As you go on stroking, that feeling of warmth is increasing. Now stroke the warts themselves. As you stroke these warts, you will feel the warmth concentrating in the warts. The warts feel warmer than the rest of your hand. They also will tingle.

"As the warmth and tingling spreads into your warts, they will gradually become smaller, they will shrink and become flatter and will gradually disappear with no scarring.

"With every hypnotic treatment that you have, your skin will become healthier. The roots of the warts will shrivel and the warts themselves will gradually wither away leaving no scars.

"You are steadily losing your desire for warts."

CHAPTER 16

HOW TO FIND A QUALIFIED HYPNOTHERAPIST

❖

I HAVE ALWAYS been a great advocate of formal scientific training. Perhaps my degrees in biochemistry, dentistry, and counseling psychology favorably predispose me in this direction; but all prejudice aside, education does serve a purpose. In an ideal world, your prospective hypnotherapist would be trained in psychology and/or medicine, but many of the techniques practiced today find no formal counterparts in the traditional curricula.

In the absence of this training, or even in its presence, certain criteria for evaluating a clinician should be employed. First, clinicians should never, under any circumstances, require recreational drugs, especially hallucinogenic agents, as part of their therapy. The purpose of hypnotherapy is to bring energy into balance and raise its quality. No drug can do that for you.

If a therapist refuses to disclose the names of former patients, do not be alarmed. Confidentiality is part and parcel of professional therapy, and in fact enjoys statutory protection in all 50 states. However, your prospective clinician should not exhibit "plaquephobia." By this term I mean an explicit aversion to having anyone closely inspect the degree(s) mounted on the wall. If a clinician advertises the trappings of a formal education, what could be wrong with examining the plaques exhibited to attest to same? Natural curiosity would impel us to study a professional's background accreditation. The problem is that if these are phony, spurious degrees purchased from a diploma mill, the hypnotist will not want you to discover this particular skeleton in their closet.

As far as bona fide degrees are concerned, a psychiatrist holds an M.D. degree; a psychologist, a Ph.D. or Psy.D. or Ed.D. (Doctor of Education); counselors usually have an M.F.C.C., M.S., or M.A. degree; social workers earn an M.S.W. or D.S.W.; pastoral counselors can have any combination of these degrees or possess a D.D. (Doctor of Divinity); dentists hold a D.D.S. or D.M.D. degree. Make sure the university the practitioner claims as his or her alma mater is accredited. Your local library can help you find this out quickly.

Remember, there is no such thing as an accredited master's or doctorate in hypnosis. The initials R.H. (Registered Hypnotist) or C.M.H. (Certified Master Hypnotist) means absolutely nothing. Anyone with the proper funds can purchase one of these "degrees" or certifications. Therapists obtain degrees in clinical or counseling psychology; marriage, family and child counseling (M.F.C.C.); social work; educational psychology; etc., not hypnosis.

Always inquire what the letters are after the hypnotherapist's name. A person with no title before his name and no letters following has to be doubly ready and willing to answer questions regarding his qualifications to instruct in autohypnosis. There are a number of reputable lay hypnotists who have compensated for their lack of academic degrees by developing a high level of skill and know-how. Those who have supplemented their hypnotic ability with a good knowledge of psychology may be qualified to do this work. Most of this group avoid doing anything along the lines of therapy except under qualified medical supervision; they limit themselves to instructing, to technical problems involving the induction of hypnosis, and to helping in the attainment of social, educational, cultural and other non-therapeutic aims. It is a deplorable fact that there are many overenthusiastic, poorly trained hypnotists who will undertake to teach "all comers" the art of self-hypnosis for a fee, assuring the applicant that success is just a matter of willingness on his part (willingness, I suppose, to pay the fee).

Your clinician should be knowledgeable about all aspects of hypnosis and be able to answer all your questions, offering appropriate guidance as needed. If it dawns on you that you know more than the therapist does, it is time to leave immediately.

A few questions to your prospective hypnotherapist can help you make up your mind:

Q: Do you guarantee that your hypnosis will work?

A: This is a very important question. No ethical practitioner ever makes such a guarantee. If your prospective hypnotherapist does, do not work with him or her.

Q: Who is ultimately responsible for my healing you?

A: You, the patient. A hypnotherapist can only train you to access your own subconscious mind and natural healing energies.

When it comes to choosing a therapist, always trust your instincts. If he or she is qualified but you don't like or trust him or her, terminate the relationship.

It is admittedly difficult to direct prospective patients to a suitable hypnotherapist. In most large metropolitan areas there is no lack of practitioners. Unfortunately, most of them are of questionable ability and reputation. The purpose of this section is to ease your search for a clinician.

Be wary of one-shot cures by a prospective hypnotherapist. It is rare that a patient with any significant issue can be treated in less than five sessions. All ethical hypnotherapists should teach self-hypnosis. This discourages dependency on the clinician and encourages empowerment on your part.

Psychiatrists tend to scoff at hypnosis due mostly to the prejudice incurred during their training and their exposure to Hollywood's version of this field. Because of the great difficulty involved in arriving at this selection, the following procedure is highly recommended:

1. Contact the local medical society. They will often have the name of one of their members who use hypnosis.

2. Ask your family physician. He or she may not use hypnosis, but often will be able to provide you with a referral.

3. Contact the local psychological association. You are more likely to find one of their members who practice hypnotherapy.

4. Scan the bookshelves of your local bookstores. Very often the author of a book on self-hypnosis can refer you to a colleague in your local area.

5. Contact the psychology department of your local university or community college. They will often know of someone you can call.

6. Ask your friends or family. You would be surprised how many people you know have been to a hypnotherapist. Word-of-mouth referrals are almost always the best type.

Please do not randomly pick a name from the Yellow Pages. This is the last resort and if you must do so, ask several questions to make sure you and he or she will be compatible. By all means, keep away from stage hypnotists and those "practitioners" who happen to hit town with a traveling show.

By the end of the initial interview both hypnotist and student should have been able to appraise each other and to have obtained a fair estimate of each other's possibilities. Often the beginnings of a good interpersonal relationship are established at this session. Now they are ready to proceed to the next step.

I hope these guidelines will be helpful to you in choosing your hypnotherapist. Ideally, they should help you avoid making a serious mistake. In the event you are already involved with a therapist who is not likely to help you, I trust you will be enabled to cut your losses and move on like the empowered soul you will become.

For those people who feel hypnosis is unscientific and is scoffed at by the medical profession, I have included the following report summaries by the British and American Medical Associations.

The British report is published in the Supplement to the *British Medical Journal* for April 23, 1955. The British Committee found:

1. There was a great deal of criticism and skepticism from medical societies directed towards those who first practiced hypnosis in Britain. This arose from the use of hypnosis for entertainment and also exaggerated claims of its medical effectiveness. The Committee deplores the use of hypnosis for entertainment.

2. The Committee finds that hypnosis is of value in the treatment of psychosomatic disorders and psychoneuroses.

3. It was also determined that hypnoanesthesia has a place for surgical, dental and obstetrical purposes.

4. Hypnosis should only be used within the competence of the practitioner.

5. A knowledge of hypnosis should be given to medical undergraduates during their psychiatric course.

6. Further research in the field is greatly needed and desired.

The report of the American Committee is in the *Journal of the American Medical Association* for September 13, 1958, Vol. 168, No. 2.

The Committee found that:

1. There are proper uses of hypnosis in the hands of properly trained physicians and dentists.

2. Each practitioner should use hypnosis only within his own area of competence.

3. There is a severe lack of training facilities for hypnosis in the United States, and that such training centers should be established under the auspices of universities.

4. The use of hypnosis for entertainment is condemned.

5. One member of the Committee took the position that there are dangers in the use of hypnosis, but other consultants were unable to support this position.

6. More research is needed to further delineate the usefulness of hypnosis.

CHAPTER 17

FINAL THOUGHTS

SELF-DOUBT AND "forgetting" to regularly practice self-hypnosis are the main obstacles to change and growth. Monitoring your progress too closely also acts as a deterrent to success. It is best not to expect too drastic a change, especially in the beginning. The long standing issues you may have will take longer to reprogram out of your awareness.

Frame your desires and suggestions in clear, short, and easily understood sentences. Use the scripts I have included as models but, by all means, modify them to suit your individual needs.

In watching for results from the suggestions you have given yourself, it is important to remember that there is frequently a time lag between suggestions being given and their fulfillment. Sometimes it is necessary to continue suggestions for some time before their effects are noticed, for frequently inner resistances has to be overcome. If it were not for this fact, all suggestions, both good and bad, would become immediately effective.

Be on your guard for a short time after having successfully achieved a change in habit. In an unguarded moment, before the new habit has become firmly established, it is easy to slide back. Carry on with your suggestions for a few days in order to consolidate the position. For example, if, through suggestion, you have given up smoking, it would be wise to continue for a few days to suggest: "I have given up smoking and *will not* smoke again. *I will not* be caught off guard when someone offers me a cigarette. *I will not* be talked into smoking," etc.

The intelligent application of self-suggestion calls for careful thought and constant revision of suggestions. It is a means to an end. You are the only one who knows the particular difficulties and problems you are faced with, the disabilities, habits, and attitudes you wish to rid yourself of, and the life you desire to live in the future. To attain these ends it may be necessary for you to reshape your suggestions frequently, guided by what is learned during self-observation.

As a result of self-observation some people find that they don't have the time to carry out exercises. Others find that they forget to carry them out. If these obstacles arise, some action should be taken. It is only by facing facts that we can alter ourselves. The majority of resolutions people make are forgotten, for the line of least resistance is to do today what we did yesterday, and most likely we will do the same tomorrow. Habits are strong, and persistence is necessary to effect change. If you should suddenly realize that you have forgotten to carry out an exercise or something you had planned, close your eyes and mentally repeat, very rapidly, to yourself: "I will not forget....I will not forget....I will not forget." Spend a minute or two doing this.

If something disturbs or upsets you during the day, take what practical action you can to deal with the incident and its possible consequences. To prevent its repetition, put the matter from your mind; suggestions dealing with it can be framed later when you are replanning your suggestions. To banish difficulties from your mind consciously is not necessarily a harmful repression, for there are "permissible repressions." The golden rule in suggestion technique is *no forcing*. Gentle persistence is the key.

Waking suggestions are carried out by repetition and can be made at any time. It does not matter where you are. Standing, walking, or sitting, once the technique is grasped, it is no longer necessary to isolate yourself. In the beginning it is necessary to have the most favorable conditions, but later all this is unnecessary. Many people who have mastered self-suggestion never go into a trance to register suggestions in their minds. All they do is close their eyes and register the desired suggestion. It would have value if the reader pauses at the end of this paragraph and says to himself (and means it) "I *am* going to learn how to get more control over my mind....I *am* going to do this."

It is a good practice to carry out waking suggestions by the integration of the subconscious activities with the conscious, intellectual activities.

Do not be uneasy or doubtful about "coming to" or "waking up" from any of the states of consciousness that are induced. Before you begin exercises, estimate what time you have available. Just think to yourself, "I've got half-an-hour to spend" (or whatever the period may be). Impress the thought on your mind, and carry on with your exercise. If the conscious mind has forgotten the time, your subconscious will remind you.

When practicing your self-suggestion sessions do not be uneasy about going into a very deep trance. If this does happen, the experience will be somewhat similar to that of dropping off to sleep. The deep trance state will turn into a normal sleep from which, after a brief rest, you will wake in a perfectly normal manner.

It is essential to direct suggestions towards the removal of negative attitudes that have arisen as a result of reverses or disappointments. From day to day incorporate in your suggestions, varying ideas to the effect that your exercises will yield progressive benefits.

When making suggestions to yourself, take your time, express them aloud or mentally. The thoughts must flood the whole mind to the exclusion of everything else. There must be no thinking, no analyzing, no self-observation about whatever you are saying: no self-criticism. All the thinking and all the analyzing should have been done beforehand. Make and accept the suggestions you are putting to yourself, with conviction. Give yourself up to the belief that what you are saying is so, in every respect. The more you are able to surrender yourself to these suggestions, the stronger your conviction will grow.

Self-hypnosis is a means to an end. The life of any individual should be lived, arranged, and organized in full waking consciousness. Self-hypnosis and suggestion are only a means of building the habits necessary to live in a healthy, balanced manner.

Never forget that pain and fatigue are nature's signals for attracting our attention. Suggestions should not be used to cancel out these signals before ascertaining other causes. Do not remove symptoms of pain or fatigue unless you are sure it is wise to do so. Always obtain a medical opinion regarding any suspicious or persistent pain or symptom.

Bear in mind that unexpected circumstances may arise that will interfere with or upset the arrangements you have planned for practice sessions. Should temporary setbacks of this nature be encountered, remember that you are no longer dealing with your difficulties with the simple outlook of someone who believes he must either be a success or a failure, but with the enlightened outlook of someone who knows his limitations and is overcoming them by consciously choosing suggestions that determine his attitude of mind and actions. Someone who is not letting chance and circumstances choose them for him. With this thought in mind, do temporary setbacks really matter ... as long as the goal is eventually reached?

INDEX

A
abstract conditioning, 21
age regression, 24, 93-97
alcoholism, 122-123
allergy, 118-119
alpha mental level, 13, 15
American Medical Association
    (AMA), 12, 130
amnesia, 23
animal magnetism, 10
anxiety, 71-72, 117-118
    -producing value, 75-76
    -provoking symptoms, 81
approach concept, 78
arm-levitation technique, 50-52
arthritis, 122
asthma, 119
astral bodies, 10
attainment programming, 9
attention fluctuating, 71-72
automatic writing, 24

B
Barbarin, de, 10
Barbarinists, 10
bed-wetting, 124-125
behavior modification, 74-77
Bernheim, Hippolyte, 11
beta mental level, 13
    returning, 135-136
blushing, 123-124
Braid, James, 11
brain
    memory trace, 17
Breuer, Josef, 11
    innovation, hypnotic therapy, 11
British Medical Association (BMA),
    130
British Medical Journal, 130

C
catalepsy, 10, 22, 80-81
Charcot, Jean Martin, 11

child induction techniques, 52
clinicians, 127
    female vs. male, 30
confidentiality, therapy, 129
conscious mind, 9, 13, 17, 19, 70, 78-
    79, 88-89, 136

D
Davis and Husband classification, 28
    chart, 29
daydream, 15
deepening techniques, advanced
    dissociation method, 68
    ideomotor signaling technique, 68-
    69
    repetition, 66-68
    Vogt's fractionation technique, 66-
    67
deepening techniques, basic
    arm-heaviness, 63
    arm-levitation, 62-63
    counting and breathing, 62
    performance and depth, 61-62
    progressive relaxation, 64-65
    step goals, 61
deeper sleep, 67
deeply relaxed. See relaxed
deep trance, 57, 58
defense mechanisms, 9
dehypnotization, 18, 23, 66
De la Suggestion, 11
delta mental level, 14
dental fear, 109
dental office visit, 110-112
desensitization process, 75
desensitization, systematic, 74
discomfort, physical, 71, 73
dissociation, 23-24
    theory, 29-30
dominant emotion, 26
dream control, 118
drug treatment method, 11
Du Sommeil, 11

ABOUT THE AUTHOR

❖

DR. BRUCE GOLDBERG holds a B.A. degree in Biology and Chemistry, is a Doctor of Dental Surgery, and has an M.S. degree in Counseling Psychology. He retired from dentistry in 1989 and has concentrated on his hypnotherapy practice in Los Angeles. Dr. Goldberg was trained by the American Society of Clinical Hypnosis in 1975 in the techniques and clinical applications of hypnosis.

Dr. Goldberg has been interviewed on shows hosted by Phil Donahue, Oprah Winfrey, Leeza Gibbons, Joan Rivers, Regis Philbin, ABC Radio, Art Bell, Tom Snyder, Jerry Springer, Jenny Jones, and Montel Williams; by CNN, CBSNEWS, NBC, and many others.

Through lectures, television and radio appearances, and newspaper articles, including interviews in *TIME*, *The Los Angeles Times*, and *The Washington Post*, he has conducted more than 35,000 past life regressions and future life progressions since 1974, helping thousands of patients empower themselves through these techniques. He gives lectures and seminars on hypnosis, regression and progression therapy, time travel, and conscious dying; he is also a consultant to corporations, attorneys, and local and network media. *The Search for Grace* was made into a television movie by CBS. The award-winning *Soul Healing* is a classic on alternative medicine and psychic empowerment. *Past Lives–Future Lives* is Dr. Goldberg's international bestseller and is the first book written on future lives (progression hypnotherapy).

Dr. Goldberg distributes cassette tapes to teach people self-hypnosis and to guide them into past and future lives and time travel. For information on self-hypnosis tapes, speaking engagements, or private sessions, Dr. Goldberg can be contacted directly by writing to:

Bruce Goldberg, D.D.S., M.S.
4300 Natoma Avenue, Woodland Hills, CA 91364
Telephone: (800) KARMA-4-U or (800) 527-6248
Fax: (818) 704-9189
Email: karma4u@webtv.net
Web Site: www.drbrucegoldberg.com

Please include a self-addressed, stamped envelope with your letter.